2/14/2009

MW00936542

Thank you

Beverly
2009

Heaven or Bust:
Journey to Glory

A Treasury of Devotional Reflections

Beverly Clopton

authorHOUSE®

AuthorHouse™
1663 Liberty Drive, Suite 200
Bloomington, IN 47403
www.authorhouse.com
Phone: 1-800-839-8640

First published by AuthorHouse 1/6/2009

ISBN: 978-1-4389-0733-8 (sc)

Library of Congress Control Number: 2008911272

Printed in the United States of America
Bloomington, Indiana

This book is printed on acid-free paper.

In Loving Memory Of

Earl, Momma, Daddy, Elliot, Ms. Lit, Winnie, Malik, Margo, and Richard

Dedicated To

My loving and faithful husband, Earl, who finished the work the Lord had for him in January, 2008, and joined my great cloud of witnesses on the other side; my children, daughter in law and grandchildren: Quentin, Miata, Katrica, Brooklin, Jordan, and Logan; my siblings: Eldridge, Christa, Harriette, Joseph, Lillie, Portia, David, Elliot, Don, Russell, and Cynthia; their spouses and my nieces and nephews; my mentor-teacher-friend, Dianna; my "companions on the way": Donna, Beverly, Dianna, Lena, Sarah, Olga, and Hattie; my aunt Lillie Ruth; my prayer team sisters, Hannah's Descendants Inc.; my Disciple classmates and students; and the "Sistuhs Who Read."

Beverly K. Clopton
Tyrone, Georgia USA 2007

Preface

"For I know the plans I have for you," declares the Lord, "plans to prosper you and not to harm you, plans to give you hope and a future. Then you will call upon me and find me when you seek me with all your heart..."

Jeremiah 29:11-14

The journey began long before it started. I believe this because I believe the words of Jeremiah 29:11-14. Long before my unconventional birth in the front bedroom of my grandfather's house, with just my mother, her sister and the doctor present, the Lord had plans for this journey. At the time, no one knew. For those present, I was just a little chocolate blessing with wide open eyes and a head full of black hair. That mother was unwed is her story, not mine. Once I arrived, according to momma and auntie, I was lavished with everything and assumed to be the best and brightest. Treated as special throughout childhood (with some adjustments being made as momma married the man who would be my daddy and they added brothers and sisters to my universe), I grew believing I was destined to achieve whatever I desired. What I eventually desired was to be a writer.

After receiving my undergraduate degree in English, I can recall as if it were yesterday a conversation with my mother. I had been home a few days luxuriating in doing nothing when she asked, "What kind of job are you planning to get?" My answer: "I'm going to be a writer. Her response: "You can't make money doing that. It's not a job. You have to get a real job to support yourself." So, dutiful daughter that I was, I applied for work at the post office and the school district. I passed both qualifying tests. The school district called first and I took the assignment to teach English just days before the post office called with a mail carrier offer. Writing took a back seat as life took over and plunged me head long into relationships and experiences that probably surprised even God. I can imagine Him saying "Beverly, this is not in the plan I've mapped out. What in the world are you doing now?"

Attempts to write were infrequent and always underscored with the sure knowledge that one day I would write the next great American novel full of love and suspense and passion. I loved the printed word and read all kinds of stuff (good and bad) all the time. Books were my passion and often my escape. Marriage, health issues, betrayal, divorce, relocation, soul mate discovery, remarriage, graduate school, parenthood, professional successes, book club and sorority friendships, church and community involvement, parental loss, retirement, another relocation, spousal loss. The "stuff" of life filled my hours. Writing was sporadic; efforts to publish unsuccessful. Eventually, journaling became a refuge and a calming cure for whatever ailed me. Still I was not yet in that plan set out for me by the great "I AM", the one who promised to give me hope and a future.

As testament to God's faithfulness and his abundant love, I was in my fifth decade before I began to understand the journey he intended for me to take. In 2001 a dear sister friend in Christ introduced me to the Disciple Bible Study Program. During year one of the four year study, I finally got it! The Lord had known me from the jump start of conception and the plan for my life was always there just waiting for me to discover it. With the help of the Holy Spirit, I understood that He gave me the desire to write. He gave me the inspiration, the revelation and the insight to put the words together in ways that would encourage others. Not the great American novel did he purpose for me. No. I have come to understand and accept His will for me is not tied to fantasy or fiction. I hear Him clearly saying, "Write, Beverly. Offer words of comfort, encouragement, and challenge. Speak to my faithfulness, my grace, my mercy and my unfailing love. Testify and use the examples and reflections I reveal to you as you learn to listen even more intently for my voice." The journey has indeed started. Come with me in these pages of reflective testimony. Savor the goodness of our Lord.

Table of Contents

Trust in the Lord with all your heart
And lean not on your own understanding;
In all your ways acknowledge Him,
And He will make your paths straight.

Proverbs 3:5-6

A Healing Tongue

Reckless words pierce like a sword, but the tongue of the wise brings healing.

Proverbs 12:18

Has an idea ever popped into your head, and without any reflection upon what you were about to say, you uttered that thought to someone who promptly received it as hurtful? Usually when this happens, we attempt to explain our intent with even more words and ultimately deepen the wound. Such experiences are typical for those who do not grasp the power of the tongue. I've written before about this small organ that can create all kinds of havoc when not controlled. I come back to the subject because "tripping on our tongues" is something we seem to do more often than not. Usually, we mean no harm when we speak. But when we give little or no thought to the potential impact of our words, we risk alienation rather than conciliation, tearing down rather than building up.

1

To avoid the chaos our tongues have the potential to create, we are challenged to grow wiser in its use. Sometimes silence really **is** golden, as the old proverb states. Not all thoughts or responses have merit; it is wiser to leave them unspoken. At other times, a word of encouragement or support is just what a person needs to bring healing to a painful experience. And, let's be honest. There are times when only a word of rebuke or correction is fitting. In any of these situations, wisdom is the key to uttering the "fitly spoken word." For the wise person allows God to order her tongue. She doesn't speak without forethought and certainly not without prayer for the right words. She rejects the "instant come-back" or the "first-strike". Her words are as deliberate and as purposeful as they are fitting. Instead of piercing, they bind; instead of cutting, they soothe. The words of the wise are filtered to remove any residue of pain. The tongue of the wise is the tongue of God.

Question for reflection: When was the last time your words brought pain? Brought joy?

Antidotes to Worry

"Therefore I tell you, do not worry about your life, what you will eat or drink; or about your body, what you will wear...Who of you by worrying can add a single hour to his life...Therefore do not worry about tomorrow, for tomorrow will worry about itself..."

Matthew 6:25-34

In an adult Bible study class one evening, as students shared their understandings of what it means to trust God and have faith in His promises, someone said, "I'm still a worrier." The person explained that though she understood the concepts of having faith and trusting the Lord, when it came right down to it, she still had a tendency to worry about "stuff" as she tried to deal with it.

That comment resurfaces in my mind whenever trust and faith testing situations arise. I think all believers in Christ will concur that we comprehend what the

3

Bible teaches us about faith and trust. It is not lack of understanding that tethers us to our worry balls. No, what stymies us is our inability to relinquish control of our "stuff" to God's capable hands. Worrying feeds our sense of self-sufficiency. During our formative years, momma and daddy, pop-pop and big momma tried to teach us to take care of our problems ourselves. Naturally that solution process includes some worrying. That's just how life is.

Perhaps this attitude is understandable in the new believer, but for those of us who have tasted the goodness of the Lord for some time, clinging to our worry balls is not an option. May I suggest three simple antidotes. First, dust off that prayer bench. Inconsistent, haphazard prayer will not develop your ability to trust God. Seek the Master's face and his Spirit during daily, intentional prayer time. The more you pray, the less you worry. Secondly, set aside time for regular study of God's Word. Enroll in a tested Bible study program like Disciple. Reorder your priorities to include Scripture time every day. The more His Word infiltrates your mind, the less you worry. Finally, learn to be still and spend time in reflection. Reflective time is quiet time, stillness time, and centering time. Your time alone with God and his Word (Psalm 46:10) as you meditate upon its application to your life. The more reflective you become, the less you worry.

As believers we accept Christ's words in chapter six of the Gospel of Matthew. We understand worry contradicts our faith and trust and we act on that understanding. We bind worry from our lips, our minds, and our hearts. We sever its cord and send it back to the enemy of our faith from whence it came.

Question for reflection: Are you still weighted down by worry or have you learned to truly trust God in all your circumstances?

Are You Ready?

Preach the word; be ready in season and out of season.

1 Timothy 4:2

Anyone who's been a Christian for a while has heard it said that the faithful are expected to "be ready". In the lyrics to a popular gospel hymn, the singer stirs our emotion when she says, "I want to be ready when Jesus comes." When the disciples asked for signs of the end of the age, Jesus told them to keep watch and "...be ready, because the Son of Man will come at an hour when you do not expect him." In the parable of the ten virgins, Jesus again emphasized that the disciples were to be like the five wise virgins who were prepared to meet the bridegroom, not like the five foolish ones who took their lamps but did not take the necessary oil to light them. Because they were unprepared when he came, they missed him altogether.

Yesterday during service, Jesus again emphasized through His servant, one of our ministerial interns, how important it is for His followers to be ready, especially when they have no idea a call is coming. The associate pastor scheduled to preach lost his voice after the first service. Both the senior pastor and senior associate pastor were away. As the associate and three intern pastors lined up to process into the sanctuary, the associate pastor turned to the young minister-in-training and said, "I need you to preach." With no more advance notice than this, the intern pastor demonstrated his readiness by rising to the occasion and preaching the morning's sermon, his Bible his only resource and reference.

Later in the day I thought about how confidently the young pastor stepped to the pulpit, and after explaining why he was there, proceeded to deliver a message to which at least one person responded by joining the church. I realized that his demonstration of readiness is what God expects of all of his followers, both clergy and laity. When we least expect it, we may be called and we are to be ready. Ready to offer unplanned hospitality. Ready with Scripture and other words of encouragement when someone calls for comfort and support. Ready to leave the comfort of home and serve the homeless when the call for volunteers goes forth. Ready to stand firm in our faith that God is in control even though our world is collapsing around us. Yes, without excuse, without hesitation, without second thought, we are to be ready.

And what enables this readiness? We can take our cue from the young pastor's introductory remarks to his selected text for his sermon. He had been studying that Scripture for some days because he thought it would be one of encouragement for his ailing father. It was his practice of reading and studying his Bible on a regular basis that enabled him to preach Sunday morning. He was ready because he was prepared. The same holds true for us. When we pray unceasingly, praise continually, and study our Bibles faithfully and consistently, we too will be ready for whatever comes. Be it a call to service or an unwavering spirit in the midst of life's storms.

Question for reflection: What are you doing consistently to be sure that when the call comes, you will be ready?

Close to God –
Great the Challenge

…Let us throw off everything that hinders and the sin that easily entangles, and let us run with perseverance the race marked out for us. Let us fix our eyes on Jesus…Consider him who endured such opposition from sinful men, so that you will not grow weary and lose heart.

Hebrews 12:1-3

When you pass the neophyte stage in your faith journey, certain clarity sets in. This march toward eternity you so joyfully embraced is not going to proceed without its twists and turns. In fact it seems the more miles you travel, the rougher the road gets. Some spots are down right hairy!

The writer of the Hebrews passage wrote of Christ's sufficiency to the persecuted Christians of his day. He wanted them to understand that their suffering was the result of their belief in Christ. That they were not to be discouraged and give up. That others had endured and they could also.

These timeless words of faith are as relevant for us as they were for the first hearers. Once on the Lord's Road, we are called to perseverance. And as we persevere, we will find that the closer we get to God, the more obedient we are to His will, the more we practice the tenets of His teachings, the more like Him we become in thought, word, and deed, the rougher the road will become. Challenges will litter the path. Quite the opposite of what seems more logical - "If I'm walking in God's will, I should be enjoying only the rewards of life." The race marked out for us isn't necessarily logical. And why should it be. Jesus' decision to leave the splendor of heaven for the squalor of a sin-sick world doesn't compute as logical either. Yet, He did. So our march to eternity is not going to be tribulation-free. The more we follow God's map quest, the harder the devil will work to get us to detour from the Savior's road. The Hebrew writer provides us with our solution. Every time the evil one erects a barrier, we throw it off. When sin ties us in knots so that we are unable to take the next step, we pause in prayer to allow God's fingers to untangle them. When distractions on the roadside tempt us to leave the path God has marked, we keep our focus on Jesus. And when the road's incline seems unending, we take solace from the encouraging words of the apostle Paul (2 Corinthians 4:7-9). God's extraordinary power enables us to gird our determination and shake weariness from our shoulders. We stay the course even more closely because we know we are traveling the only road worth taking - the Lord's Road to Eternity.

Question for reflection: Are you on salvation's road or are you taking a pathway that leads elsewhere?

Confident Prayer

O Lord, you have searched me and you know me.
You know when I sit and when I rise; you perceive
my thoughts from afar...you are familiar with all
my ways. Before a word is on my tongue, you know
it completely...

Psalm 139:1-4

This Davidian Psalm is an inspiring reminder of God's omniscience, omnipotence, and omnipresence. The writer David most certainly speaks to the attitude every believer ought to bring to prayer time. Unfortunately, this is not always the case. Sometimes, we find ourselves approaching the throne of grace with great hesitancy instead of confidence. Like the four year old trying to summon the courage to say, "I did", when mom screams, "Who broke the lamp?" This Scripture reminds us that we worship and serve a God who knows everything. We may try to peek from around the corner, hoping not to get caught, but nothing we think, say, or do is hidden from Him. More amazingly, He even knows the words we are trying to form before they leave our mouths.

Understanding the extent of God's knowledge, His power, and His presence frees us from the self-imposed barriers we bring to prayer. What need for mental censoring before a God who perceives our thoughts from afar? Why the wasted time grappling for the precise words before a God who already knows what we are tying to say? And why any pretense about our motives before a God who is thoroughly familiar with our ways?

When we fully comprehend this God who knew us before conception and set the number of our days before we began living them, we can pray with confidence anytime, anywhere about anything. His knowledge of us is such that our prayer attitude ought to be fearless. No timidity on bowed knees for us. Knowing that God knows the outcomes already ought to boost our assurance. With boldness born of the certainty of who He is, we can pray with confidence. We believe that because He knows us, He will act in our best interests.

Question for reflection: Do you tip toe through your prayer time or do you pray with both feet on the ground?

Connected to the Power Source

"But you will receive power when the Holy Spirit comes upon you, and you will be my witnesses in Jerusalem, Judea and Samaria, and to the ends of the earth."

Acts 1:8

These words of Jesus, spoken to His followers just before He ascended into heaven, were just what they needed to hear from their Savior. The declaration assured them they would be receiving power from God to continue the ministry Jesus had begun. They understood the might of this power for they had witnessed Jesus use it to bring comfort, healing, forgiveness, and wholeness to many during His three year journey to the cross. When the Holy Spirit came to rest upon them as recorded in chapter two of the Book of Acts, they were instantly connected to the power source that would enable them to fulfill the Lord's command.

When those of the Christian faith accept Christ Jesus into their lives and profess their belief in Him as the resurrected Son of God, they too are connected to the power source. When Christians observe Lent, the forty day period in which they practice self-denial and self-examination in preparation for the celebration of resurrection Sunday, it is a perfect time for an examination of the status of the connection to be sure they are receiving the promised power.

For some, these forty days will reveal that their power source connection is secure, a snug fit of cord to outlet. Their spiritual disciplines of daily prayer and devotion, consistent study of God's truth in His Word, quiet moments set aside to listen to His voice, and faithful service for others that glorifies Him alone keep their connection to the Master in place. Alas, for others, the examination will reveal their connection is more like that of the cell phone user who travels through "dead zones" and experiences "dropped calls" at crucial moments. Their connecting cord is frayed, loose, partially pulled out, or just lying on the floor beneath the outlet - within reach, but unplugged. Having forsaken the spiritual disciplines necessary to maintain the connection to their Lord and Savior, their lives reflect their powerlessness.

The joy of the Lenten season of denial and reflection is that it offers continuing hope and the promise of restoration and renewal. During this period, the faithfully connected are able to grow even more fully into the disciples Christ calls them to be. Those who find themselves disconnected are granted yet another chance to turn back to Jesus, to pick up the cord, examine it and do whatever repairs are necessary to reconnect it to the outlet. For only when truly connected to the power source, God Himself, are Christians able to fulfill their mission of witnessing "to the ends of the earth".

Questions for reflection: What's the status of your connection? What can you do to secure your spiritual cord?

Countenance Witnessing

Jesus came to them and said…"Therefore go and make disciples of all nations…teaching them to obey everything I have commanded you…"

Matthew 28:18-20

He said to them, "Go into the entire world and preach the good news to all creation."

Mark 16:15

He told them…. "You are witnesses to these things."

Luke 24:48

As the Gospel writers record Jesus' final instructions to his followers, we get a clear picture of his expectations for them. They had been witnesses of who He really was, and they were to make disciples of others by witnessing to what He had taught them. Though we may not be eyewitnesses like the eleven to whom Jesus spoke these

17

words before His ascension, we are charged with the same mission He gave them. These 2000 years later, His message has not changed. We are witnesses and we are called to witness.

Somehow, though, we twenty first century believers in Christ struggle with the "how" of Jesus' commission even as intellectually we understand the "what". For many, witnessing is what missionaries do. They witness when they take the Gospel message to non believers in far away places with funny names. To fulfill Jesus' command, we must shift our thinking. We don't typically talk to others about our experiences of God's grace in our lives as our witness to who He is. And we shy away from sharing these experiences as inroads for others to accept Him. We leave stuff like that to the preacher.

Perhaps one of the easiest ways we can overcome this hesitancy and witness our faith is by our countenance. One of the Merriam-Webster dictionary's definitions of *countenance* is "the face as an indication of mood, emotion, or character." Aha! The light bulb comes on. Yes, our countenance is often a window to who we are. We don't have to be in another country. In our homes, our workplaces, our churches, anywhere we are, we can witness. If we claim we are followers of Christ, we can witness to our faith with our countenance. A facial expression that exudes friendly warmth rather than brittle coldness, eyes that sparkle with joy rather than glower with distain, and an overall look of calmness in the midst of chaos and confusion. Such a countenance draws others to us and opens the door for us to share what God has done and is doing in our life. It paves the way for the telling of the "good news of Jesus Christ."

So being a witness and witnessing is more than missionary work. Every morning above ground the opportunity to adhere to our Savior's commission awaits us. After the soap and water and the astringent and moisturizer, our countenances are ready to "witness to these things." to a searching world.

Question for reflection: What does your countenance say to the world about your faith?

Culture or Christ

No one can serve two masters. Either he will hate the one and love the other, or he will be devoted to one and despise the other. You can not serve both God and man.

Matthew 6:24

It's a thought to ponder daily - what is the effect of contemporary culture on our faith? How does its influence cause us to compromise what we profess to believe? Without knowing it, we who claim Jesus Christ as the resurrected Son of the one living God, are often snared by its power. One of the reasons this happens to us is because so much of our culture is woven into our religion that we don't know where the divide ought to be. We embrace "politically correct" positions on issues that contradict Scriptural teachings. We allow the power of the popular media to dictate what is valuable when it relates to what we wear, where we live and how, what we drive, where we send our children to school, what organizations we join, what causes we support, what we accord worthy of our attention. On the surface it would seem there is nothing wrong with this way of living.

Unfortunately, for Christians what this lifestyle represents is a surrender of our beliefs by attempting to live in two worlds. Our faith teaches us that this is impossible. The Word is clear that if we love (embrace) the world, we hate God. We can not serve two masters. For us each day demands a vigilance usually reserved for times when we are physically threatened. With the same degree of alertness and wariness we would employ for those times, we must evaluate everything in our cultural experience to judge that we are resisting anything that denies God's absolute sovereignty in our lives. Perhaps our constant question should be: "Does this choice or decision please God?" We remember that no one knows the day or the hour when Christ will return. We can not afford to be partakers of the non-Christian aspects of our culture if we claim Christ as our victor. We are called to be ready, lamp lit, to stand before Him assured of his blessing. We say "No" to the temptations of culture today to insure His "Yes" to us in that great tomorrow.

Question for reflection: Are you ready for Christ's return or does the "culture" still ensnare you with its compromises?

Disciplined Tongues

All kinds of animals, birds, reptiles and creatures of the sea are being tamed and have been tamed by man, but no man can tame the tongue. It is a restless evil, full of deadly poison.

James 3:7-8

The Bible study lesson was about our use of the tongue. The Scripture reference was the familiar one from the third chapter of the Book of James that speaks of the difficulty we experience in taming the tongue and the negative effects that result when we do not. As Christians we ask ourselves if the speech we utter, enabled by our tongues, reflects our faith. Does how we talk contradict what we claim we believe?

All too often we easily forget that what we say can be as deadly as any weapon built to maim or destroy. In public or private conversations, words, unless guarded or "tamed", can cause pain and grief. Our challenge is to learn to speak the truth in love, to use speech to uplift and encourage and to bless. The tongue which enables speech is to be used in ways that glorify God, that lead to the building of His kingdom, that witness to His majesty and power, His grace and mercy and love. As we learn from the Scripture, we do none of these things when, with our tongues, we both praise God and curse men. Our tongues when used to do both become hypocritical, undisciplined instruments.

We are wise to remember that something so small as the tongue can yield awesome results. If left unchecked, it poisons and destroys the fruit we seek to produce. But if disciplined, it can produce a harvest beyond measure.

Question for reflection: Who rules your words? You or your tongue?

Divinity Lamps

"You are the light of the world. A city on a hill cannot be hidden. Neither do people light a lamp and put it under a bowl. Instead they put it on its stand, and it gives light to everyone in the house. In the same way, let your light shine before men, that they may see your good deeds and praise your Father in heaven."

Matthew 5:14-16

This familiar metaphor Jesus used during His sermon on the hillside near Capernaum is as relevant today as it was then. His words challenge us to examine whether we are intentional in how we live. Are we mindful in even the mundane to allow the light of Christ in us to shine as a beacon to others? Or are we so consumed with our secular pursuits and responsibilities that Christ's light is shadowed, filtered, or worse yet completely obscured? Have we who Jesus calls "the light of the world" turned our dimmer switches to a faint glow?

When we entered into a personal relationship with the Father through His son Jesus Christ, we became His divinity lamps. His words define our function as light givers. Just as we employ manmade lamps to brighten dark places, Christ uses us as His lamps to illumine His promises in our daily walk. When the light of the Good News shines in us without interference, we show God to those who walk in darkness. When our words, our actions and behaviors reflect Christ's Spirit, we bring hope to those who struggle to find their way. When we position ourselves so that others see the unwavering light of Christ in us even during our personal trials and sorrows, we proclaim to them our absolute faith in God and his sovereignty.

Yes, as Jesus' "divinity lamps", we keep our dimmer switch turned to its brightest setting. We know this is the only way to bring Him honor, to be truly His lights in the world.

Question for reflection: What is the status of your lamp? Opaque? Filtered? Shaded? Or Shining Brightly?

Encounter at Starbucks

"Come follow me," Jesus said, "and I will make you fishers of men." At once they left their nets and followed him.

Matthew 4:19-20

On yesterday, the Lord reminded me again of what it means to "leave our nets" and follow Him. In between doctor appointments, my husband and I stopped at Starbucks. It's not a place we frequent often, but we had time to kill. Inside it was quiet and cool, a welcomed respite from the searing Atlanta heat. As we sat comfortably sipping our lattes, a woman entered. By the trembling of her shoulders, I knew she was in distress and probably crying. She chose a table across from us and I saw the tears streaming down her face. I asked, "Are you all right?" She replied, "My youngest brother just died." Before I could say anything else, an apparent friend arrived at her side and began to comfort her. They both finally sat and the friend continued to speak softly. I prayed silently. After several minutes, I felt I should do more, but I hesitated. I reasoned that the grieving woman had an obvious close friend; both were making phone calls regarding passports and airline tickets. Things were under control. Maybe my silent praying was enough. Just as that thought crossed my mind, the woman burst into fresh tears and I could clearly see the pain etched in her face. I felt the prompting of God's Spirit urging me forward to their table, but a new negative pushed to the front. "Maybe they're not believers." The Spirit countered, "So what, you are." And with that, I found myself moving out of my chair. With the courage that only the Lord gives, I approached them and said, "I'd like to pray for her." The friend seemed startled, but the grieving woman's eyes gave permission. With a slight nod of her head, she bowed as I held her and began to pray, softly aloud, unmindful of those who sat at tables around us. The Holy Spirit gave the words and I spoke them as I asked God to comfort and bring peace to this, His child and her family, to replace their sorrow with His joy in Jesus' name. No other words passed between us and I finished praying as her cell phone rang. As my husband and I left, a man sitting by the door smiled at me.

When I reflected later on this encounter with a stranger at Starbucks, I realized several truths. First, when we commit to follow Jesus, we have to leave our nets behind. Often our nets of pride, of not wanting to appear foolish, of possible rejection, of being embarrassed by what others think can keep us tangled, out of step with God's will for us. Christ calls His followers to bold witness, to stepping out on faith and trusting Him to provide what we need to do kingdom work. Secondly, when we commit to follow Jesus, Satan will always try to divert us with his arrows of doubt, anxiety and fear. Jesus expects us to serve Him through our service to others. As the Samaritan ministered to the man on the Jericho road, we are called to minister love and mercy to those we meet in our daily walk. Finally, when we commit to follow Jesus, we commit to a life of faith manifested in our actions. We don't just verbally profess our faith, we live our faith. We leave behind the net of religiosity for a genuine relationship with the living Lord. And that relationship won't allow us to sit quietly on the sidelines of life. No. That relationship with the divine pushes us out of our comfort zones, net less, into the fray and service of the Lord.

Question for reflection: How many "nets" still entangle you and hinder your service to the Lord's kingdom?

Everlasting Comfort

"Do not let your hearts be troubled, Trust in God; trust also in me. In my Father's house are many rooms; if it were not so, I would have told you. I am going there to prepare a place for you. And if I go and prepare a place for you, I will come back and take you to be with me that where I am you may be also."

John 14:1-3

Recently, a friend shared a quote she read that touched her spirit. The speaker was Tony Snow, the White House Press Secretary who had a recurrence of cancer spread to his liver. In an address to students at his alma mater, Davidson College, he stated, "I am actually enjoying everything more than I ever have. God hasn't promised us tomorrow, but he has promised us eternity."

Mr. Snow's optimistic remarks remind us that God's Word, the Bible, is filled with promises that sustain and comfort. Even the "situational" believer can locate Scriptural passages that offer solace or encouragement during times of crisis or challenge. There is nothing that touches human life to which God has not spoken words of assurance. The promise of salvation (Matthew 1:21), of peace (John 14:27), of the Holy Spirit (John 14:16-17), of forgiveness (Psalm 103:8-10, of joy (John 15:10-11), of strength (Ephesians 3:20). These promises enable us to face life's ups and downs, bends and curves with hope instead of desperation. Mr. Snow's paraphrase of John 3:16 is the promise that equips us to struggle through our trials and tribulations with a spirit of joy rather than sadness. We can refocus from the temporal to the eternal when we accept this promise of comfort that knows no time constraints.

Yes, the everlasting comfort of our heavenly Father strengthens our resolve to hold on; it banishes our fears and supports us as we live in the confidence of our convictions. To the unbeliever or doubter, our joy in the midst of affliction seems strange, perhaps a little crazy. But our ability to persevere in praise is possible because we worship a God whose word we "can take to the bank." John 3:16 says it all: "For God so loved the world that he gave his one and only Son, that whoever believes in him shall not perish but have eternal life." Is there any greater comfort than that promise? Christ's disciples don't think so.

Question for reflection: When faced with desperate situations, do God's promises comfort you to the point that you don't lose hope?

Exam Time

Examine yourselves to see whether you are in the faith; test yourselves.

2 Corinthians 13:5

These words of the Apostle Paul to the church at Corinth may seem odd upon initial reading. They did to me. For many, the words "examine" and "test" usually summons images of all-night cram sessions before the dreaded final examination. Students take these exams to demonstrate to the teacher their mastery of course content. I don't know anyone who subjects himself to the process from a personal desire for self-evaluation.

Paul's advice in this Scripture suggests that perhaps self-examination or self-testing is just as important as being tested by someone else. As believers, we have come to understand and accept that God is our master examiner. He allows circumstances to touch our lives as a way of testing our faith and trust in Him. He holds both the answer and scoring keys for every exam. Paul seems to be saying, however, that we who claim Christ ought to be doing some periodic self-testing, not just waiting around to be tested. Taking little mini exams to better prepare us for the Lord's next chapter quiz.

By testing ourselves, we discover whether our words, our thoughts, our actions are in line with God's Word. Self-testing our faith walk on the journey allows us to make the adjustments necessary to keep us in line with God's will. Self-examination prepares us ahead of time for God's inevitable testing time. When He hands out the next exam and says, "You may begin." we are better positioned to withstand what may appear incomprehensible at first. But closer analysis should reveal that our self-testing is paying off. We know how to deal with the sorrow, the tragedy, and the pain. Our faith is strong. The discipline of continual self-testing of our faith prepares us to respond to life's exams with absolute trust and hope in God alone.

Question for reflection: Have you developed the habit of regularly self-testing your faith? If not, why?

Eyes Fixed on Jesus

Let us fix our eyes on Jesus, the author and perfecter of our faith, who for the joy set before him endured the cross…. Consider him who endured such opposition from sinful men, so that you will not grow weary and lose heart.

Hebrews 12:2-3

Though the writer of this New Testament epistle may be unknown, he (or she) provides renewed focus for the believer who is often sidetracked by the world's beckoning. Not on the popular main streets of fame and fortune, or the beguiling avenues of acquisition and possession is the believer called to walk. The Master's expectation is that the faithful instead will traverse the "road less traveled" and view the world through the same servant lens as He.

With eyes fixed on the Savior, the believer sees the children, birthed yet not nurtured, clothed yet exposed to depravity, fed yet hungry for innocence and wholesomeness. The believer sees the outcast - the beggar, the blind, the homeless, the abused, the mentally deficient, the overworked and underpaid. And because his eyes are properly focused on Jesus, the one who introduced the life style, not of the rich and famous, but of the faithful servant, the believer shuns the temptation to look the other way. He accepts the risks, the inconvenience, the rejection, the ridicule, and the shaking of the heads in disbelief as he sets about doing the work Jesus calls the faithful to do.

Because his eyes are fixed on our Lord, the believer's weariness does not linger. He recovers from any missteps, confident that the Lord will provide. His fixation on the Savior provides enduring strength for the journey toward salvation.

Question for reflection: How do you keep your eyes fixed on Jesus as you walk this pilgrim's journey?

Faith Amnesia

Then Jesus said to his disciples: "Therefore I tell you, do not worry about your life, what you will eat; or about your body, what you will wear...Who of you by worrying can add a single hour to his life? Since you cannot do this very little thing, why do you worry about the rest...O you of little faith...your Father knows that you need them. But seek first his kingdom, and these things will be given to you as well."

Luke 12:22-31

Jesus' words about the futility of worry are familiar to all Christian believers. On a cerebral level, we understand both the words and their meaning. We are not to worry or be anxious about anything: neither life itself nor the provisions necessary to sustain it. God knows our needs and will provide for them. Simple enough, right? But in the meantime, the baby still needs shoes, the rent is past due, the tires on the car are shot, the company just cancelled employee health benefits and the twins are due next month, and the food in the pantry never seems to last until pay day. Kind of hard "not to worry" about these things and simply wait around for God to provide.

What is the believer to do? How do we cease being "worry warriors" of little faith? Let me say first that it isn't easy, even for the long term Christian. Our humanness easily clouds our vision and our acceptance of God at His Word. We forget we are both flesh and spirit. I call this tendency to forget, "Faith Amnesia." It makes us think we are in control. It leads to faulty thinking that in turn produces doubt, anxiety and worry. *What are we to do? Where is the money coming from? How will I ever be able to handle this?* Faith Amnesia questions.

As believers, we must focus on the key elements of Jesus' remarks to His disciples in this passage. Worrying does not equip us to change anything. God's provisions extend to all His creation. God knows our needs more keenly than we do. And most importantly, our focus must be upon God Himself, His kingdom and His will. As believers we make the connection between "little faith" and "much worry." We banish this faulty thinking by turning our concerns over to Him even as we continue the struggles of the day-to-day. We pray our belief that what may appear a dismal situation is already resolved in the heavenly realm because we believe "faith is being sure of what we hope for and **certain** of what we do not see (Hebrews 11:1 - Emphasis mine). As believers each day we mature more fully into a faith-filled" little flock" that moves about life's pastures confident in God's provision for our needs. Our motto becomes: "More Faith. Greater Trust. Less Worry."

Question for reflection: Do you tend to suffer from Faith Amnesia when life's struggles seem beyond your control?

Follow the Leading

...At that time you will be given what to say, for it will not be you speaking, but the Spirit of your Father speaking through you.

Matthew 10:19-20

...Make the most of every opportunity.

Colossians 4:5

My husband and I agreed. The Seven Last Words of Christ Service was phenomenal. Each of the pastors from the seven churches stood and proclaimed a stirring Good Friday message based upon one of Christ's seven utterances from the cross.

This morning as my thoughts drifted back to the service, I realized I had witnessed first hand the power of God's Holy Spirit at work. The pastor who was scheduled to preach first from Luke 23:34 ("Father, forgive them") was unable to get to the church. The host pastor so informed the congregation as the service began. Then he referred to the twenty-second chapter of Genesis where Abraham was about to slay his son Isaac. Whereas it was the host pastor's responsibility to fill in for any missing-in-action pastor, God had stepped in at the last minute and provided him a "ram in the thicket." Minutes before the ministers were to walk into the sanctuary, he had spotted a fellow pastor not on the program sitting with the congregation. Without hesitation, she said, "yes", to his request for her to preach Christ's first words.

In her white robe (all the other ministers wore black), she stepped to the pulpit from her seat and you sensed the Spirit's hand upon her. Before she began her sermon, she shared her experience prior to getting to church. As she made her preparations, the Spirit spoke and told her to take her robe. She put her robe in the car. Then It told her to take her Seven Last Words booklet. She put it in her purse. God revealed His purposes when the host pastor "arrested" her as she sat waiting for service to begin. Because she was available, ready, and willing, God enabled her to speak boldly to the theme of Luke 23:34. The power of the Holy Spirit resting upon her, she made the most of this opportunity to testify to God's power and grace.

We don't have to be ordained ministers of the Gospel for God to use us in similar fashion. In fact, His will for us, no matter our spiritual gifts, is that we simply be available when He calls. That we learn to listen for the leading of His Spirit. That we stay prepared, in and out of season, to speak the truth of our faith, to share the good news of the Gospel in any circumstance. If ever there was a demonstration of God's Spirit at work in the here and now, it was this pastor's unscheduled preaching at this service. In her obedience, God used her in a mighty fashion. He seeks to do the same in our lives, as we grow more faithful in making the most of the opportunities He sets before us. As we learn to discern the leading of His Spirit. As we simply say, "Yes", to His call.

Question for reflection: When He calls, will you be ready?

Forgiveness

Then Peter came to Jesus and asked, "Lord, how many times shall I forgive my brother when he sins against me? Up to seven times?" Jesus answered, "I tell you, not seven times, but seventy-seven times."

Matthew 18:21-22

The theme of forgiveness was the concept explored in a recent devotional I read. As I reflected upon it, I realized how easily we recite, "Forgive us our trespasses as we forgive those who trespass against us.", but how difficult it is to actually live these words day in and day out. When we transgress God's law, we go to Him in prayer and expect to be forgiven. But when others "sin" against us, we struggle with forgiving them. In fact, the whole concept recedes in our minds and hearts as resentment, anger, dislike take center stage.

As Christians, we are summoned to a higher calling. We can not afford the luxury of an unforgiving heart. The Scripture is clear. We forgive others as often as it is necessary. We do this because we understand that the One who died on the cross for our salvation continues to forgive our sins. He demands no less of us in our relationships with others.

Question for reflection: What do you do to counter the temptation to hold grudges against or not to forgive someone whom you feel has harmed or offended you?

Framing Tomorrow

Therefore do not worry about tomorrow, for tomorrow will worry about itself. Each day has enough trouble of its own.

Matthew 6:34

At first reading, the title, "Framing Tomorrow", and the familiar verse from the Gospel of Matthew would suggest a contradiction. After all, if we are admonished to not worry about tomorrow, then what is the need to "frame" it? Yet, it is precisely because we know that each day presents its own ups and downs that we find purpose in "framing" the one yet to come. What I have come to appreciate is the notion that we frame our tomorrow by what we draw today. Think with me for a moment.

As believers, we agree with James' advice in his epistle to the first century Christians. He reminds them in chapter four that they should avoid boasting about what they will do because they have no idea what will happen tomorrow. Only God sees beyond the next moment of our lives. Our tomorrow may herald the heady celebration of dreams come true, the painful reality of sorrow's touch, or the gradual onslaught of physical or mental infirmities. No matter. It will be the frame around each experience that defines how we live in that moment. And we construct those frames by the "drawing" of our faith.

When we "draw" a fervent, unceasing prayer life, we frame a tomorrow of trials and tribulations with trust and hope in the Savior's deliverance. When we "draw" an unselfish spirit of serving God by serving others, we frame a tomorrow of our needs being met more abundantly than we could ever imagine. When we "draw" a spirit of obedience to God in all things, we frame a tomorrow of joy and peace that surpasses all understanding. When we "draw" a life that never stops worshipping the Lord, we frame a tomorrow with grace sufficient to meet us at our points of need.

So, we do not worry about tomorrow. Instead, we draw it today with what we will need to sustain us when it comes, a frame sturdy enough for whatever that unseen canvas holds.

Question for reflection: What do you need to work on to better frame your tomorrows?

From Struggling to Knowing

Then Jesus said to his disciples, "If anyone would come after me, he must deny himself and take up his cross and follow me. ...What good will it be for a man if he gains the whole world, yet forfeits his soul? Or what can a man give in exchange for his soul?

Matthew 16:24-26

"What can a man give in exchange for his soul?" As Christians we know the answer is "Absolutely Nothing." Yet despite knowing this truth, we still struggle with the issue. We tend to get ensnared in wanting the things of the world: possessions, status, influence, success, recognition, wealth. It is so easy that often we are not even aware that we have surrendered our knowledge of the truth. We say that God wants to bless us with His prosperity and the desires of our hearts. We read these words in Scripture and interpret them to mean we should have all the world offers.

Perhaps, however, our failure to resist this lure of worldly things is related to our lack of understanding of what God means by "prosperity" and "desires of the heart." I submit that neither has anything to do with the material or secular. Rather, I think it means God wants to bless us with those attributes that He knows will lead us to eternal life: love, joy, peace, kindness, patience, self-control, faithfulness, gentleness, and goodness - the Fruit of the Spirit. Possession and use of these things will guarantee God's prosperity. Likewise the "desires of our hearts" are to be those things that bring us closer to Him. He wants us to desire in our hearts to worship Him, to praise Him, to honor Him, to give Him thanksgiving, to love Him. He is worthy and the desire of our hearts is to acknowledge His worthiness in all we think, say, and do.

Quite different than the secular understanding of "prosperity" and "desires of the heart" are these understandings. Yet, this is exactly what we must know and do if we are to be called followers of Jesus Christ.

Question for reflection: What must you do to close the gap between your knowing the truth and struggling to live it?

God's Apprentices

For we are God's fellow workers....

I Corinthians 3:9

Do your best to present yourself to God as one approved, a workman who does not need to be ashamed and who correctly handles the word of truth.

2 Timothy 2:15

My devotional this morning dealt with faith and how we demonstrate it by trusting God to handle our situations and leaving it up to Him to do what needs to be done. The key point made was that we should just go on about our business, not trying to help God with the issue, knowing that He's got it under control. This kind of attitude manifests our faith.

As I pondered the message, with which I basically agree, a thought occurred to me. Suppose God wants us to demonstrate our faith by not only bringing the concern to Him, but also by allowing His Spirit to direct us toward the solution. Scripture tells us that we are His fellow workers and workmen. Perhaps our work with Him sometimes means we demonstrate our faith and trust in more concrete ways. Not with distrust in His power to deal with a situation, but, when led by the Holy Spirit, in an active participation with Him.

I don't know. The devotional message seems a more passive one and somehow God doesn't strike me as a proponent of passivity. As His earthly coworkers, He may want us to give the broken item to Him to put back together, but not to leave the workshop unless He so directs. As His apprentices, He just might choose to use us in a particular situation as tools of encouragement, instruments of peace, or models of love as He does the work of reparation. If our attitude is to dump our concerns at the door, wipe our hands, and walk away, we might be missing the link between faith and action. As I said, I don't know, but it is a thought.

Question for reflection: Do we just wait on the Lord or work with Him as His Spirit directs?

Going Through the Motions

Do not merely listen to the word, and so deceive yourselves. Do what it says.

James 1:21

I've said it before. I'll say it again. Staying true to our faith is not easy. The temptation is strong to conform to the morality of the times, and just go through the motions of being a Christian. We think, "Who will know? Who will care?"

The struggle for faithfulness is not new. Our biblical ancestors faced the same dilemmas and often became quite expert at "going through the motions." In their complacency and accommodation to foreign cultures, they spent their time and resources in selfish pursuits. They did this even as they continued to observe their religious rituals: feasting, fasting, congregating, bringing offerings, and making music unto the Lord. Their outward displays of piety belied the truth of their lives - worshipping the gods they made for themselves and the idols of their time. But God knew their duplicity and hated their self-centeredness (Amos 5:21-27)

Like our ancestors, many of us abandon the truth of our faith. Like them, we become quite skilled at "going through the motions." We go to church, put our offerings in the collection plate, stand and sing the hymns, and applaud the morning message. From all outward appearances, we are a religious people. But God knows us. He sees what we do with our time, the talents He gave us, and the resources He provides. He knows our hearts. He watches as we pass by on the other side of the road to avoid the fallen stranger. He churns inside when we blame the victims of poverty for their plight. He bristles when we close ranks within our communities, churches, and social organizations to keep out those who aren't like us. And He hates our self-absorption and willfulness.

Yet, as He did with our biblical ancestors, God continues to care about us. He wants us to be doers of His Word and not just hearers or pretenders. He seeks an authentic relationship with us, one that strengthens us for the faith journey, one that keeps us true to His will and purpose for our lives. Praises to a God who never gives up on us, even when we are "going through the motions."

Questions for reflection: Is there a gap between what people see and what God knows of your faith journey? What can you do to close it?

Good Intentions

"But I did obey the Lord," Saul said... "The soldiers took... the best of what was devoted to God, in order to sacrifice them to the Lord your God at Gilgal." But Samuel replied, "Does the Lord delight in burnt offerings and sacrifice as much as in obeying the voice of the Lord?"

1 Samuel 15:20-22

As much as we want them to be, our good intentions are seldom enough when it comes to a righteous relationship with our God. Saul's intention to offer the plunder from his victory as a sacrifice met neither God's standards nor his commands. Samuel declared Saul's self-perceived good intentions as disobedience of God' will.

As faithful Christians, we must guard against this Saul-like behavior. Our intentions noble, but not in obedience to God's will and purposes. Most of us live daily with the best of intentions to be good followers of Christ. We know the lifestyle to which we are called. We comprehend the Ten Commandments; we understand Jesus' theology of caring for the sick, the bereaved, the lonely, the stranger, the homeless, the prisoner; we grasp the significance of hospitality and generosity as hallmarks of our faith; we appreciate the practiced discipline of praise and worship, Bible study, and prayer. Yet, often, our intention to do God's will in these arenas of our lives remains just that _ an intention.

For a myriad of reasons, we don't make that leap from intention to obedience. We intend to. When the time is right. When some of the work commitments are out of the way. When the children are grown. When dad gets better. When the promotion comes through. When...When...When. Excuses rationalizing our disobedience. So we never get around to making that phone call to the sick and shut-in, visiting the nursing home, sending that card of encouragement to the young man incarcerated, adopting that child, attending that Bible study class, inviting that new family to dinner, taking that food basket to the shelter, writing that check for victims of the war, building that Habitat for Humanity house, volunteering to read at the elementary school. The list goes on.

Saul's fateful encounter with a God who demands obedience, not sacrifice, reminds us that when we live our lives filled with good intentions and never transform them into obedience to God's dictates, we, like Saul, will be judged accordingly.

Question for reflection: What's keeping you from translating intentions into obedience?

Guns and Generators

You will keep in perfect peace him whose mind is steadfast, because he trusts in you. Trust in the Lord forever, for the Lord, the Lord, is the Rock eternal.
Isaiah 26:3-4

Under the caption, "Make My Day", the Hurricane Katrina survivor stood posed for the camera wearing dark eyeglasses and holding a stub-nose 38 Smith and Wesson gun in one hand. The newspaper article reported that the New Orleans resident feels confident now that she owns both a gun and a powerful generator. She's ready for the next storm or the dangers of the city's escalating crime rate. Her expression seemed to say, "Bring it on. I have the resources to handle it."

At first I was amused by the pluckiness of this woman in her sixth decade. No shrinking violet, this Southern Belle. However, my amusement soon turned to sadness as I continued to stare at the picture. Despite what the Clint Eastwood quote implied, neither the

Smith and Wesson handgun nor the high-powered generator will guarantee the peace from turmoil the sexagenarian seeks.

As believers in Christ Jesus, we pilgrims understand that natural and manmade challenges are always just around the next bend in the road. In many instances no matter how we prepare, they cannot be avoided. We also know that nothing man makes can provide ultimate protection from these forces when they strike. Neither can man-concocted solutions spare us the turmoil or chaos that surrounds the trials and challenges. Only with God can we know perfect peace in the midst of tragedy. Only when we depend upon him for our protection and security can we face the perils of life unshaken by their threats.

A snub-nose gun may scare someone away, but it may not. A generator may keep the power going for a while, but it won't run forever. Only an all-powerful God is able ultimately to offer us eternal steadfastness and stability during life's tribulations. That is why we place our trust in him, not in guns and generators.

Question for reflection: What keeps you balanced when life's storms threatened your peace and security?

Hosanna! Hosanna!

The crowds that went ahead of him, and those that followed shouted, "Hosanna to the son of David. Blessed is he who comes in the name of the Lord. Hosanna in the highest."

Matthew 21:9

As the beginning of Holy Week signals the close of another Lenten season, Christians reflect again upon the close of Christ's earthly sojourn. On Palm Sunday, we hear the familiar Scripture recounting Jesus' triumphant entry into Jerusalem. Though He rode on a lowly donkey, not the prancing white steed of a conquering king, the crowd shouted their "Hosannas" with the hope that this miracle- worker and teacher was indeed their long awaited Messiah. The one who would deliver and restore them. With little understanding of Scripture and refusal to accept Jesus as its fulfillment, in a few days hence they watched on the sidelines as their conquering hero was led to a cross, crucified with common criminals. We can only imagine what they thought as they stood there, watching salvation unfold at Calvary, and not comprehending its significance. With shoulders shrugging and heads shaking sadly from side to side, were they simply resigned to Jesus' fall from hero to crucified? Did they turn away and begin the walk back their villages thinking, "Well, I guess He wasn't the Messiah after all. Too bad though, He certainly seemed like He was with all those miracles He's been performing. But He wasn't able to save even Himself from the cross, so He surely must not have been the one we are waiting for."

With resurrection eyes, we easily accuse these early followers of Jesus. Surely, we say, they should have understood by His teachings and His deeds who He was. Their "Hosannas" should have been as loud as they stood at the foot of the cross, as they were when they were on the road with Him to Jerusalem. After all, His crucifixion was about to release them from sin's wages and grant them eternal life.

May we be reminded however, that in many ways we are not unlike our faith ancestors. We shouted with joy and sang praises in His honor when we first accepted Him as our Lord, our Savior, and our Redeemer. For many miles, we traveled before and after Him, clapping and waving our hands, singing His praises, reading His Word, listening as the minister taught and preached from the pulpit. More than we like to admit though, when situations in our lives seemed too difficult to bear, we gave way to despair.   Like the early followers, we shrugged our shoulders, shook our heads in dismay and turned back to our villages, the places we were when we first heard His call. Sadly, we thought, "I gave that religion stuff a chance, but look what has happened to me. Jesus has not saved me from all this. He must not be who He claims He is."

Scripture doesn't tell us how many, if any, of those Jerusalem-road celebrants eventually accepted Christ, as the apostles continued to spread His message. But we contemporary followers who have accepted His call cannot deny our biblical history. Christ arose from the dead. He ascended back into Heaven from which He came. Our belief and faith in His defeat of death and His divinity demand that we reconnect to His promises no matter how difficult life's challenges and trials. On Easter, Resurrection Sunday, we proclaim loudly, "Hosanna! Blessed is the one who came in the name of the Lord. Blessed is our Messiah, Jesus the Christ!"

Question for reflection: Are you still shouting, "Hosanna, Hosanna" no matter what circumstances come your way?

Imitation or the Real Thing

So they took the bull given them and prepared it. Then they called on the name of Baal from morning to noon. "O Baal, answer us!" they shouted. But there was no response; no one answered. And they danced around the altar they had made. At noon Elijah began to taunt them. "Shout louder!" he said. "Surely he is a god! Perhaps he is deep in thought, or busy, or traveling. Maybe he is sleeping and must be awakened."

Kings 18:26-27

Today we chuckle at the image of the prophets of Baal dancing around his altar, calling his name and hearing no response. How silly, we think, that these prophets would actually expect something man-made or man-inspired to hear and respond to their needs. God's prophet Elijah adds to the absurdity of the scene with his taunts that perhaps Baal is not answering because he is thinking, busy, traveling, or sleeping. Later in the

Scripture (1 Kings 18:28-39) when the one true God responds to Elijah, his prophet, with omnificent power, there is no doubt in anyone's mind who the true God is and whom they should worship.

At the risk of offending, I suggest that we are not all that different than the prophets and people who worshipped the powerless, man-made and man-inspired god Baal. Think about it. Here we are, post resurrection people who have the benefit of history and knowledge that God alone is omnipotent. Yet, we still seek other gods to satisfy our needs, wants, and notions of prosperity. We call on our gods of technology, status, possessions, appearance, politics, education, and achievements. The list can go on. You get the point. Bowing to and serving these man-determined sources of power and providence make us just like the ancient prophets and the people who believed in and worshipped the god Baal. Even with our salvation secured by Christ's ultimate sacrifice, we continue our worship of imitation gods. What will it take for us to recognize the one true God as the only one to be worshipped? Was not His display of power and might on Easter Sunday morning superlative enough to make us exclaim daily "The Lord, He is God! The Lord, He is God! (1 Kings 18:39). Elijah's God, our God, has already done more than enough for us. No other gods should be worthy of our consideration.

Question for reflection: What modern-day gods do you still call upon to meet your needs?

"In His Way, In His Time"

"Do not be afraid, Zechariah.... Your wife Elizabeth will bear you a son..."
Luke 1:13

The title phrase above stopped me this morning during my own devotional time. I came across it in the commentary related to the story of Zechariah and Elizabeth. As Zechariah performed his priestly duties, the angel Gabriel spoke to him. He revealed God's will that his barren wife Elizabeth would bear him a son. With them both being advanced in age, Zechariah voiced his skepticism. The reward for his unbelief was instant muteness that was not reversed until after the child's birth.

The story caused me to step back mentally from some troublesome family issues and recognize that God hears my spoken prayers for His intervention. He even hears my unvoiced thoughts about the situations. He knows the weight of these issues upon my heart and spirit. He knows I want Him to act now, to do something to make things right. He also knows that my feeble attempts to fix the problem will end up just as my biblical ancestor Sarah's when she devised her own solution to her barrenness (That great idea only enflamed the situation. Genesis 16).

What the commentary phrase reminds all of us as believers is that God is an on time God. Though it may seem our prayers are falling on deaf ears, that we're not getting through or worse yet, that we're being ignored, God will respond to us. What we must remember is that we are not "the boss of God." He is the one in charge, in control of His universe, His world. He responds to every concern lifted to Him in His own time and in His own way. So, when we're praying for loved ones to change or for familial challenges to be conquered, we must be mindful, and even encouraged that God knows. The situations are not "Breaking News" to Him. Not only does He know the problem, He knows the when, where, and how of the ultimate solution. And that is where we find our comfort, our joy, and our release.

Question for reflection: When the problems just keep mounting and the answers remain illusive, how do you respond?

In Jesus' Name

…. That if you confess with your mouth, "Jesus is Lord," and believe in your heart that God raised him from the dead, you will be saved…
"Everyone who calls on the name of the Lord will be saved."

Romans 10:9, 13

Last evening's conversation with a dear friend still resonates this morning. She spoke of those in her seminary program who criticized her again for ending prayer with the words, "In Jesus' Name" before saying "Amen." Two things stunned me: the group is Christian, and is comprised of both seminary students and others who serve in positions of leadership within the church community. Regardless of status however, they all profess Christianity as their faith. At the same time though, they think the use of the expression is inappropriate because the program is "interfaith."

At the risk of offense, I think their stance is nonsensical. How does one claim to be Christian and have a problem with acknowledging Jesus Christ in prayer? For that is exactly what you are doing if you say a prayer that does not close with the familiar, "In Jesus' Name." This kind of theology occurs when in our efforts to be all-inclusive and to proclaim ours is an "interfaith approach", we strip away the essence of our Christian beliefs. We acclimate to a trend of thought that reduces our faith to a plethora of empty litanies and rituals that do not serve the purposes Jesus Himself proclaimed.

How do you deny Jesus as the cornerstone and architect of your faith when He told His disciples (and that includes you and me) to "go and make disciples of all nations."? (Matthew 28:18-20) and to "go into all the world and preach the good news to all creation. Whoever believes and is baptized will be saved." (Mark 16:15-16). How do you follow this command or commission without witnessing when you pray or speak? How do you deny His assurance that things done in His name (Mark 16:17) and things asked for in His name (John 16:23-24) will be granted?

All of us, including those seeking ordination and those already ordained, would be well advised to revisit the Scripture, to read and ponder Jesus' words in the verses referenced above and then recall Paul's words to the church at Colosse: "And whatever you do, whether in word or deed, do it all in the name of the Lord Jesus, giving thanks to God the Father through him" (Colossians 3:17). To do any less is to deny the Christian faith.

Question for reflection: When you pray, how do you typically close your prayer? Why?

It's All for the Good

For all things work together for good for those who love the Lord and are called according to his purpose.

Romans 8:22

I love the Lord. I feel I am called for His purpose by witnessing for Him through my writing. Therefore my sitting here in a hospital lobby to be admitted for a liver biopsy procedure is an experience that I accept as being "for the good." As I await the appearance of the medical personnel who will perform this procedure, I am reminded once again of the truths of Scripture. In 1 Thessalonians, the apostle Paul admonishes us to pray unceasingly. In the book of Romans, he assures us that nothing can separate us from the love of God in Christ Jesus. In Philippians, he exhorts us to rejoice in the Lord always.

For the believer, these Scriptures are never more real than at times such as this one. Just the thought of a biopsy is frightening enough. The unknown factor of the procedure would bring anxiety to even the most ardent disciple. But when we take the Lord at His word, something marvelous happens. We approach every experience confident of the Lord's promises. When we have been diligent and faithful in our study of His Word, we know He abides with us in the treatment room. When His joy provides our strength and lights our countenance, the surgical environment is calm and peaceful creating the perfect condition for His guidance of the doctor's hands. So I am serene in my waiting, empowered by His Spirit to write of this day's experience even as it happens (and to finish before the sedative lulls me to sleep).

How awesome is the God we serve. He takes our challenges and uses them as a witness to others of how He does indeed work everything together for good for those who love Him. This is the key - to love Him. For those of us who do, everything is as it should be.

Question for reflection: Do you love the Lord enough to trust Him completely with whatever challenges come your way?

Joyous, Patient, Faithful

Be joyful in hope, patient in affliction, faithful in prayer.

Romans 12:12

These words of encouragement from Paul to the believers in Rome continue to inspire Christ's followers today. In them he captures the key to living a life of faith no matter the circumstances of the actual day-to-day journey.

Telling us to "be joyful in hope" implies that we will occasionally be challenged by one of life's inevitable trials. Perhaps the test results are positive and the cancer treatments must begin immediately. Maybe six months have elapsed since the lay off notice and the only jobs available are outside your area of training. Living in hope for adverse circumstances to change is not easy. And to remain joyful during these times is especially difficult. But for believers, Paul's words must be taken literally. Hope without joy defeats us. If the joy of the

Lord is indeed our strength, then we have what we need to continue. His strength fills us with joyfulness as we await with hope His victory in our trial.

Encouraging us to be "patient in affliction" is a simple affirmation of our faith. We embrace patience as a desirable fruit of the Spirit. It enables us to endure suffering to "wait patiently for the Lord" like the palmist David, until He hears and responds to our cry.

And patience during times of torment leads us naturally to Paul's third admonition to be "faithful in prayer." It is usually during life's afflicting moments that we surrender ourselves to God in prayer. These times bring us quickly to our knees in supplication before His throne. Sometimes, though, despite our whispered entreaties or anguished cries, no answer comes. Believers understand that this may very well be "testing time." Sometimes God's silence is the way by which He stretches us to even greater faithfulness. By our refusal to stop praying, we demonstrate our complete trust in Him. For faithfulness in prayer is one of the foundations of our beliefs. We pray without ceasing because this religious discipline bolsters our hope, keeps our joy complete, and increases our patience during difficult times. Faithfulness in prayer shapes our faith journey.

Question for reflection: Is it difficult for you to remain joyful, patient, and faithful in prayer when problems arise?

Just As He Told Them

Then came the day of Unleavened Bread on which the Passover lamb had to be sacrificed. Jesus sent Peter and John, saying, "Go and make preparations for us to eat the Passover." Where do you want us to prepare for it?" they asked. He replied, "As you enter the city, a man carrying a jar of water will meet you. Follow him to the house that he enters, and say to the owner of the house, 'The Teacher asks: Where is the guest room, where I may eat the Passover with my disciples?' He will show you a large room, all furnished. Make preparations there." They left and found things just as Jesus had told them.

Luke 22:7-13

Amazing isn't it, how you read a familiar Scripture passage and a new understanding suddenly springs to mind. For a moment you pause and ponder, and then you smile, thanking God for his continuous revelations and inspirations.

Such was my experience this morning as I read the Luke passage above. The Scriptures that recount Jesus' final journey to Jerusalem and the cross are certainly not new. Like most Christians I have read them many times. This morning, however, I realized this particular passage provides us a demonstration of Jesus' omniscient divinity that may often go unnoticed. It didn't involve an overt miracle, but rather something quite ordinary. In His words to His disciples about preparation for the Passover meal, He revealed this divinity in a very mundane circumstance. Consider the following:

- Only an omniscient God knew that a man and not a woman would be walking in the city with a jar of water headed to the house where He would have supper.
- Only an omniscient God knew that just the mention of His identity - "The Teacher" - would be sufficient for the owner of the house to provide the room for the meal.
- Only an omniscient God knew that the room would be already furnished and ready for the meal.

These revelations of God's omniscience validate our faith. They free us of anxiety and worry because they show us clearly the power of the God we serve. He knows everything and in His knowing, we take comfort and have peace.

But not only did the passage affirm Jesus' omniscient divinity, it also spoke to the faith of His disciples. Notice that they posed no questions to Jesus other than to ask, "Where do you want us to prepare for it?" They took

Him at His word that things would be as He said. Now imagine for a moment such a conversation with one of us modern-day disciples.

"You sure about that, Lord? A man with a jar of water. Men don't carry water jars. That's women's work."

"You think he's really going to be okay with us saying You said, The Teacher asks"? Maybe You should write him a note so he'll know it's You and not us asking for this room."

"And how do You know the room there will be large enough. There are thirteen of us. And furnished already? What if it isn't? *What then?"* Amusing, but so typical of us!

Unlike the disciples in this passage, we do struggle to accept Jesus' words as truth. We question; we evaluate; we seek clarity; we call a meeting. More commonly we cover our bases with our own plans, just in case what He says falls short of our expectations. When we respond in this fashion, we're really revealing our hesitancy to accept that Jesus is indeed divine, omniscient, and still in the miracle business. We twenty first century Christians would do well to pattern this example of faith the disciples demonstrated when Jesus told them what to do.

Question for reflection: Is His word truth in your life? Is it enough for you to move forward with what He calls you to do?

Keep Praying

Pray without ceasing.
                              I Thessalonians 5:17

Over the years I have vacillated between two theologies regarding prayer. One maintains that we present our request once to God and leave Him alone to handle it; the other suggests that we bombard heaven daily with our petition until an answer comes. Each prayer approach has its supporters, faithful followers of Christ who believe their particular view is what God requires of us. Lately I have come to the conclusion that what Jesus taught His disciples specifically about persistence in prayer in the eighteenth chapter of the Gospel of Luke should be our model. Jesus tells the disciples the parable of the widow who kept going to an unjust king for justice (Luke 18:1-8). It was His way of demonstrating to them that they should always pray and never give up. In verses seven and eight, Jesus says that if an unjust king can answer a petition then surely God, the antithesis of injustice, will bring justice to His own who cry out to Him. Like the unjust king, our God will not forever delay answering our prayers. He will bring deliverance.

This model of consistent, unceasing prayer encourages us to present our petitions to our Lord daily, trusting that in time He will answer us. We are to do so without hesitation or fear that He already has heard us so we don't need to repeat ourselves. We reject the notion that He may be annoyed because we return with the same old pleas. We continue to pray because Scripture tells us that's what we should do. It's a matter of faith and trust. Like the widow in the parable, we don't give up. We come back again and again, confident that one day, in some way, God will answer our prayers. He proclaims He will in his Word and we accept that Word as a truth deposit.

Question for reflection: Which are you? A one-timer or a repeat-requester when taking your petitions to the throne of grace?

Mustard Seed Faith

I tell you the truth, if you have faith as small as a mustard seed, you can say to this mountain, "Move from here to there" and it will move. Nothing will be impossible for you.

Matthew 17:20-21

In the seventeenth chapter of Matthew, Jesus' disciples asked him why they had been unable to heal a boy who was demon possessed. Following their failure to do so, the boy's father brought him to Jesus. In what seems a mood of exasperation with the disciples, Jesus heals the boy. Later when they are alone with Jesus, they inquired of him why he could heal the child and they could not.

It occurred to me Jesus' answer to the disciples might have been different than it was. He could have claimed his divinity and said, "I am the Messiah, the Christ. Of course I can do things that you cannot.

Remember, you are man". This was a reasonable response because it was truth. But with our post biblical view, we understand that Jesus, the greatest teacher, would never pass up a "teachable moment" and this was surely one such moment. The disciples, like us, needed to truly understand "Faith" (Matthew 17:20a). Jesus' words were blunt and to the point: "Because you have so little faith". Now, the disciples, again like us, might have been offended at these words. They probably felt they had demonstrated their faith by their actions of leaving all to follow Him. Similarly we feel we demonstrate our faith by joining the church and serving in its ministries. But Jesus' exasperation with His disciples and with us comes from His knowledge that our outward professions of faith, though necessary, do not get to the core meaning of faith in Him and the Father.

In the passage noted above, Jesus speaks to the disciples as He does to us about the kind of faith He wants us to have - mustard seed faith - seemingly impossible but mighty beyond comprehension. Faith that understands the power source is God Himself. The unnamed author of these words makes this kind of faith even plainer when he writes, "Faith - to believe the task ahead of us is never as great as the power behind us." When we have mustard seed faith, we operate in full confidence that if God said we could do it, it's true and we can. Does Scripture not say, "All things are possible for those who love the Lord and are called according to his purpose" (Romans 8:28)? Our mountains are movable, but they won't budge an inch until we believe God's power expressed through our faith in Him is absolute reality.

Question for reflection: Where is your faith – floating around outside or deep inside your core?

Naked Witnessing

When Jesus had called the Twelve together, he gave them power and authority to drive out all demons and to cure disease, and he sent them out to preach the Kingdom of God and to heal the sick. He told them, "Take nothing for the journey – no staff, no bag, no bread, no money, no extra tunic..."

Luke 9:1-3

As contemporary disciples we understand that Christ Jesus calls us to evangelism, to being witnesses of the faith. Yet, when we consider His commands to His disciples in this ninth chapter of Luke's Gospel, we take pause. The idea of going on a journey of any kind without the necessary provisions of food, clothing, and money seems to us unrealistic. We ask, "How did Jesus expect them to survive?" We often conclude that this teaching is not only too hard to follow, but is simply impractical for us today. Why, we are expert travelers. We know what a journey requires. The idea of going on one without our suitcases packed, extra money in our wallets, and travel accommodations and reservations in hand is unheard of. Yes, we will go to carry the Good News message, but we'll be more prepared for the journey than those disciples. They might as well have been naked!

Perhaps we struggle with the meaning of Jesus' message in this Scripture because we fail to make a distinction between journeying for self and journeying in witness for the Lord. The journey's purpose dictates what we need to take with us. Jesus sent the disciples on a journey as the first witnesses to His divinity. They did not need the things He told them to leave behind. Without them, the reason for their journey would be more easily accomplished. With no material encumbrances, they could focus solely on the message of God's Kingdom. In their "nakedness", the people would see God's power and authority manifested in them.

It is the same for us today. As Christ's ambassadors, we witness "naked", shedding our status, our prestige, our influence, our degrees, our wealth, and our possessions. As we share the Good News of the Gospel and testify to God's amazing grace in our own lives, we allow His power, His glory, and His love to shine in and through us. We trust the Lord and His Holy Spirit to lead us and to fill us with what we need to witness to all who need to hear.

Question for reflection: At what stage are you in your call to witness?

New Christian

But grow in grace and knowledge of our Lord and Savior Jesus Christ…

II Peter 3:18

The woman referred to herself as a "new Christian" as she shared her story. Usually when a believer uses this term, the listener or reader assumes the individual is a new convert to the Christian faith. The image of "new" typically suggests the person has just recently accepted Christ and is a "mere infant", not ready for "solid food", but rather still subsisting on "milk" in the practicing of the faith (I Corinthians 3:2).

It is unsettling to contemplate the reality that there are many long time, "old" believers who profess Christianity yet are no more mature in their faith than the new convert. These "old" Christians demonstrate by their actions that they are still infants. Jealousy and quarreling continue among them. Self-boasting flows easily from their lips and pride rides comfortable on their shoulders. They justify their deeds with indignant self-righteousness. They live not as examples of the faith, but as people who themselves need someone to instruct them again in the truth of God's Word (Hebrews 3).

No matter how long the profession of faith, three months or three decades, a "new" Christian is someone who still lives on the milk of the gospel, someone who has not graduated to the solid food of righteous living and practice of the faith, someone who has not yet successfully trained herself to distinguish good from evil in all things (Hebrews 5). Someone, perhaps, like you or me- believers still struggling to throw away the bottle and pick up the spoon. Still struggling to finally make the necessary transition to Christian maturity.

Question for reflection: At what stage of Christian growth are you? Still stuck on a bottle or grasping a spoon?

Path of Righteousness

He leads me in the path of righteousness for his name's sake.

Psalm 23:3

This morning's devotional time led to the thought that the path Jesus has laid out for us is a path of righteousness. What we experience sometimes, most times, is that life's trials, pains, hurts, disappointments, and frustrations obscure the path. The resulting fog clouds the way and we find ourselves stumbling along, not sure of the direction He would have us take. How do we find our way out of the murkiness and back to the clarity and purpose God intended, back to His path of righteousness?

We intentionally pursue righteousness, even as we struggle with the murkiness. As the Psalmist writes, it is the path He chooses to lead us on. "Yes," you say, "but what is that path of righteousness?" The apostle Paul tells us in the Romans, chapter four and Galatians, chapter six, that God credits as righteousness our belief and faith in Him. When we demonstrate our belief in His Word and our faith in Him as our sovereign Lord by our willingness to live the fruit of the Spirit, we discover the path anew. The fog lifts as we strive to live these attributes daily. Miraculously, our issues are resolved, our vision clears, and the path looms ahead crystal clear. The key to staying on the path of righteousness is intentionally trusting, believing and obeying God's Word.

Question for reflection: Is your path clear or is haze causing missteps?

Do You Really Believe?

Do not let your hearts be troubled. Trust in God; trust also in me. In my Father's house are many rooms; if it were not so, I would have told you. I am going there to prepare a place for you. And when I go and prepare a place for you, I will come back and take you to be with me that you also may be where I am.

John 14:1-3

These familiar verses are often used to comfort and encourage persons facing major life challenges: incurable disease, terminal illness diagnosis, and untimely death of a loved one. Jesus spoke these words to comfort His disciples as they struggled with understanding His forthcoming death and departure. He tried to assure them that their trust in God and in Him would not go unrewarded. He would return and take them back to be in the same place with Him. Still, some of the disciples, Peter, Thomas, and Phillip specifically, continued in confusion and doubt. The actuality of His death, resurrection, and return was just too hard for them to believe possible. They struggled despite having been eyewitnesses to the miracles Christ performed.

In addition to offering us comfort today, these verses cast many of us right along side the doubting disciples of Jesus' time. Perhaps we can accept that if we trust God, our heartaches will be easier to bear. But to go to the next level and actually believe that He is coming back for us, that eternal life does exist, now that's something else all together. Like Peter, Thomas, and Phillip, we modern day disciples struggle with this promise because our belief system only goes so far. The level of trust needed to accept the truth of Jesus' words is muted by the cultural contamination of our faith. Even with post-resurrection eyes, we give only so much of Scripture relevancy in our lives. To trust at the level His words imply demands living in ways many of us reject as unrealistic. It's as if we can only accept the explainable pieces. To really believe that all of His words are truth, that He will return, stretches us to uncomfortable positions of faith. As disciples however, we have no options. We are called to believe and to witness even to the truths that fly in the face of conventional reasoning and rationale. Ours is a belief based upon trust and faith.

Question for reflection: Be honest. Do you really believe there is life after death for those who claim Christ as their Savior?

Sin Traps

"If we claim to be without sin, we deceive ourselves and the truth is not in us."

I John 1:8

"What sin traps catch me again and again?" This question posed in a recent devotional gave me pause. Sin is sin, so we are not just speaking of breaking the Ten Commandments when we consider our sins. For an example, gluttony is sin is it not? When we eat to a point beyond our need or overeat to the point where we are excessively overweight, we sin. We sin because with these behaviors, we fail to honor God's temple, our bodies, and the place where His Spirit dwells. So for many, overeating becomes a "sin trap".

Lack of faith is a sin. Consider the person who goes to God with a prayer petition and then continues to worry and fret about the request. Trying to figure out a solution to something you've supposedly handed over to God and not waiting on Him demonstrates a lack of trust in God's power to deal with everything in His time and way. The "sin trap" is one of not honoring and trusting His sovereignty, His omnipotence, the foundational concepts germane to the Christian faith.

Yet, we thank God because we have a Savior who allows u-turns. He continues to forgive us of those sins that show up only on His radar. Even as we learn to dodge one "sin trap" and slip into another, we take comfort in His abiding grace and mercy.

Question for reflection: What "sin traps" do you struggle to overcome?

Why Do You Doubt?

Immediately Jesus reached out his hand and caught him. "You of little faith," he said, "why did you doubt."

Matthew 14:31

The disciples had been with Jesus for quite some time. They had witnessed His supernatural power and authority on numerous occasions. You wonder just how many more miraculous healings of both body and spirit they needed to see before they accepted without doubt that Jesus was the Son of God. When He came to them walking on water, they had just witnessed and participated in the feeding of five thousand plus people with just five loaves of bread and two fish. Why, they themselves had collected the twelve baskets of leftovers! Yet, the sight of Jesus walking on the water filled them with dread. And though Peter initially stepped out of the boat on faith, he too fell victim to fear and doubt when the winds and waves arose.

This biblical account reminds us how easy it is to forget the miracles of our lives and the countless instances of God's providence. It's as if each day is unconnected to the one before and the experiences of God's faithfulness are unrelated. Just like the early disciples, we see the Lord work out the pain, the hardships, the suffering, and the grief to which we are prone. Still when the next trial, the next wind of adversity blows against us, we like Peter, cry out, "Lord, save me." We forget that He is truly the Son of God. He will not forsake us or leave us to drown in the dark waters of life's challenges.

We are wise to remember that at some point in the journey, He expects us to exhibit a faith that blocks doubt's influence. To know in our spirit that no matter how impossible the situation may seem, we need not fear. Our faith tank, filled with miracle memories, will provide the fuel to withstand the winds that threaten to blow us over and the waves that seek to pull us under. As believers, we claim an ever growing faith and nothing less than an absolute annihilation of doubt.

Question for reflection: What strategies do you use to counter the doubt and stand on faith when life throws its curve balls?

"How Salty Are You?"

"Salt is good, but if it loses its saltiness, how can it be made salty again? It is fit neither for the soil nor for the manure pile; it is thrown out."

Luke 15:34

The Bible lesson I was studying posed the question: "How salty are you?" in reference to the Luke Scripture noted above. As I contemplated the query, I thought about salt's natural properties and uses. Its most common use is that of flavoring, adding taste or spice to what otherwise would be bland and unappealing. For years, its preservative qualities have prolonged the usefulness of meats and other food items. In earlier times (and to some extent today), salt's ability to heal or cleanse brought relief to its users.

Jesus' statement of salt's value reminds us that we should exhibit these characteristics in our walk as disciples. As followers of Christ, our mission involves preservation. By example, we demonstrate our faith commitment to His Word. In continuing to obey and practice His teachings we preserve and pass along the heritage of our faith. We continue to be in the world, but not of the world, as we remain committed to the work of His kingdom.

Likewise as disciples, we understand that we are called to add the "spice of Christ" to our daily walk. Ours is not a bland, uninspired faith journey. Rather, as Christians we serve with joyful thanksgiving, lifting enthusiastic praise to our God for the Good News of the Gospel. In everything we incorporate Christ as the seasoning of our lives. Finally, as His followers, we offer healing to the least, the last, and the lost as we honor Him with our service to others.

Unless we display these "salty" characteristics, we have no value in God's kingdom and become only something to throw away.

Question for reflection: How salty are you in your faith journey?

Youthful Rebellion

*I will set out and go back to my father and say
to him: Father, I have sinned against heaven and
against you...So he got up and went to his father.*
Luke 15:18-20

The message in the *Upper Room* about working our
way back to God after rebellion was powerful. How
like so many of us is this man who wrote of his youthful
rebellion and "prodigal son" behaviors. I don't know
about you, but I can identify with the writer in many
ways. Although I did not turn my back on going to
school and finishing degree requirements as he did,
I did say "no" to many other teachings of my mother,
especially those involving relationships. I made my own
way giving little thought to Christian principles relative
to morality or relational covenants sanctified by God's
Word. As a result of those decisions, I paid heavy prices
that produced despair and sorrow.

But praise God, like that prodigal son, one day I woke up, looked around and realized that I had a loving, forgiving, grace filled heavenly Father who was just waiting for my return. Now I can claim victory as I walk in His path toward the life purposes He intended for me all along. As I imagine the prodigal son did, I cherish my Father's forgiveness of my youthful indiscretions and rebellion. He is always faithful, even when we are not. Alleluia, Abba.

Question for reflection: Have you made your way back to your Father or are you still swimming in a pool of rebellion?

Outcomes: Yours or God's?

When God saw what they did and how they turned from their evil ways, he had compassion and did not bring upon them the destruction he had threatened. But Jonah was greatly displeased and became angry....But the Lord replied, "Have you any right to be angry?"

Jonah 3:10 – 4:3

Consider if you will, God's man Jonah. God called him to do something he really didn't want to do, so he ran from God. Or at least he tried to. When he finally submitted his will to God's will, the outcome was not what he expected or thought appropriate. He got mad at God for involving him in the situation in the first place! Sound like anyone you know?

Often we are like Jonah. We think our plans or solutions are better suited to life's challenges than those of God. In fact when we occasionally listen to Him and act according to what we perceive He is asking, we expect the outcome to be what we wanted anyway. The story of Jonah teaches us differently. We learn that it is not our call to decide God's outcomes. He is no respecter of person and because He isn't, He hears the pleas of all who call upon Him. We are not called to judge; that's God's job. We are called to obedience. As we mature in our faith, we learn to be thankful for what He does for us without feeling anger or resentment when He also blesses those we feel are unworthy of His providence.

Question for reflection: How do you reconcile your feelings of anger or resentment when it seems those who don't deserve it are enjoying God's blessings?

Good Deeds and Eternal Life

What good is it, my brothers; if a man claims to have faith but has no deeds? Can such faith save him...As the body without the spirit is dead, so faith without deeds is dead."

James 2:14 and 26

I read today of a Christian whose belief is that good deeds are not the ticket we need to get into heaven. His theology suggests that as Christians we will want to do good deeds, but that we are not necessarily required to. By his reasoning, our tickets were purchased and paid for by Christ's death on the cross and if our faith rests upon that we will have eternal life.

Now I understand that without Christ's sacrifice and His blood spilled on the cross for us, we could not even approach heaven's gates, let alone enter them. But I also understand from Scripture that our faith requires action to fulfill our acceptance of the new covenant. To say that we do not need "good deeds" is to misrepresent our part in the salvation story. Chapter two of the book of James makes clear that faith without deeds is useless. When Abraham offered his son Isaac on the altar, his faith was made complete by his actions. When Rahab the prostitute gave lodging to the spies and sent them on a route to safety, her actions were considered righteous. Verse twenty-six of James is crystal clear: "As the body without the spirit is dead, so faith without deeds is dead."

Our acceptances of Christ as our Savior and of the new covenant His death and resurrection represent require us to demonstrate by our actions the faith we confess with our mouths. In chapter ten of the Gospel of Luke, Jesus tells the law expert that if he loves God and his neighbor as himself, he will inherit eternal life. Fulfillment of these commandments requires action, not just a pronouncement that one believes in them. Jesus gives us the parable of the Good Samaritan as an example of good deeds that give life to faith. The powerful words of our Savior in Matthew's Gospel are explicit. He calls us to go beyond believing in Him to specific action. We feed the hungry, give drink to the thirsty, clothe the naked, invite in the stranger, and visit the sick and imprisoned. These are actions that exemplify our faith convictions. Without such actions or "good deeds", Christ says we go to eternal punishment, and not to eternal life.

Question for reflection: Are you resting comfortably on your couch of faith or is yours a daily effort to be a "doer" of the Word?

The Joy of the Lord

"This day is sacred to the Lord your God...Do not mourn or weep. For all the people had been weeping as they listened to the words of the Lord. Nehemiah said, ... " Do not grieve, for the joy of the Lord is your strength."

Nehemiah 8: 9-10

In this passage from Nehemiah, the people weep openly as Ezra, the priest, reads from the Book of the Law of Moses. They grieve because they realize how disobedient to God they have been. But Nehemiah assures them there is no reason for such dismay and sorrow; the strength they need to live in accordance with the Law is already theirs. It is their joy in the Lord.

Nehemiah's words are just as prudent today. Consider the times of our weeping and mourning. We answer the doorbell and Trouble strolls in, laden with so much baggage we wonder just how long he will stay this time. We spend our years courting financial and personal success in ways that contradict our faith. Just when we finally realize only God's truth is the fulfillment of our dreams, Guilt slithers across our path, stirring feelings of shame and failure that block our reconciliation. We train the children up in the ways they should go (Proverbs 22:6), but for some reason when they leave home, they seem to lose their way. Confusion and Chaos, their new confidantes, beguile with choices too tempting for them to resist.

It is precisely in the midst of these circumstances that tear at our souls that we are called to remember Nehemiah's words: "The joy of the Lord is your strength." A primary benefit of our relationship with the Lord is the joy and peace it gives us. We can rejoice at all times because of this soul communion with Him. Joyful hearts and minds, strengthen by the positiveness of Godly-relationship can withstand, endure, struggle against, and ultimately defeat any grief-producing, tear-jerking situation that comes our way. When we claim the strength God gives us as we rejoice in Him, we approach times of weeping and mourning with celebration and praise.

Question for reflection: What must you do to cultivate greater joy in the Lord to give you the strength you need to face life's challenges?

Waiting on God

...For the Lord is a God of justice. Blessed are all who wait for him.

Isaiah 30:18

Ours is not a society of "waiters." Our hurry-up, text message, download- it-to-me-now world values instant responses and immediate actions. The idea of "waiting" suggests we are either unprepared or incapable of dealing with situations and challenges. In the blur of trying to live in the world without surrender to the world, even the Christian can forget that focused waiting is a discipline of our faith. The psalmist (Psalm 130) reminds us that in times of struggle and trial, we cry out to God and then we wait on Him. How then do we wait?

Certainly not as the world around us waits - impatient, always seeking the quick and easy answer. Rather, we understand that waiting on God is a measured soul response. Therefore, we trust His Word that no matter what challenges we face, He will not forsake us. Our faith in Him is rooted in the delivery experiences of our past. Our hope in Him rests securely in our knowledge that He cannot lie and His very Word is truth.

So, as believers, we accept the blessing for our ability to wait on Him. No whinny complaints of "Where is the Lord when you need Him?" escape our lips. We release our anguish to Him with confidence that in His own time He will answer our cries. We accept that waiting on God strengthens us for our salvation journey. The waiting toughens us for the next round of our match with the enemy. We take courage, not in the quick fix or compromised response, but rather in the soul-satisfying knowledge that whatever His answer and whenever it comes, it will be for us an answer that reveals His glory in our lives.

Question for reflection: After you've lifted a concern to the Lord in prayer, do you struggle with waiting for His answer?

Count Your Blessings

The earth is the Lord's and everything in it, the world, and all who live in it...

Psalm 24:1

The refrain to that old song runs often through my mind: *"Count your blessings. Name them one by one. Count your many blessings. See what God has don."* Often we are so busy living that we forget that life itself is a gift, a blessing. It belongs to Him, just like everything else on earth does. When He decides to bless us with life in His world, we begin a relationship with Him that demands acknowledgment of His blessings, His gifts. No matter how busy we are, we must take the time to "count our many blessings".

So we count it a blessing when:

- We open our eyes each morning clothed in our right minds.
- Our senses function and our limbs, though creaky, move us where we need to go.

- We have food, shelter, and clothing as so many others struggle daily for these basic necessities
- Our children and loved ones are safe from the perils that plaque families and communities everywhere.
- Our paychecks or other forms of compensation arrive regularly when many are without adequate financial resources.
- We worship freely in our churches and temples without the fear of reprisal faced by many believers
- We have opportunities to give back, to share, and to witness to the least among us.
- We can travel relatively free of restriction within our country's borders with suicide bombers not being the norm of daily life.
- Despite its flaws, our democratic government works for the welfare of its citizens.
- We serve an omnipotent, omniscient, omnipresent God who loves us and who demonstrated that love by sacrificing His only son, Jesus Christ, for our salvation.
- We have both God's living Word and His Spirit to help keep us in right relationship with Him.
- We live under His grace in the world as we anticipate His glory in the world yet to come.

We count it all a blessing when we consider all He has done, is doing, and will do in our lives.

Question for reflection: When was the last time you took the time to "count your blessings"? Do it now.

Divine Direction

Trust in the Lord with all your heart and lean not on your own understanding; in all your ways acknowledge him, and he will direct your paths.
Proverbs 3:5-6

Callers who reach my cellular voicemail hear me greet them with these words of Scripture. They are among my favorite for their clarity. I think of them as "divine directions" for their ability to assist us in living, as God would have us live. Our adherence to the verses reminds me of a popular cable program, "Divine Design". On the show, homeowners seek direction for solving their interior decorating challenges. Unsure of their own abilities to transform a room from shabby to fashionably chic, they place their confidence in a designer's knowledge and expertise. With little hesitation, they relinquish control and decision-making regarding everything from color scheme to room design to furniture placement to the skill of a "divine designer".

This helps them avoid costly mistakes and creates instead the perfect design for the desired living space.

The wisdom of the proverb can do the same for the Christian believer. With the realization that we need divine direction for navigating life's trails, roads, and highways, we can go to our divine designer, the one waiting on the other end of our "On Star" prayer button. We can confess the doubts and fears that keep us from figuring out the best plan for our earthly sojourn. We can say to Him:

"I don't know what I'm doing. My ideas aren't working out. Nothing seems to fit the design I drew. I need some direction, some expertise to figure out which way to go. I need your power to direct my steps. I need you, Lord, only you."

And like the interior decorator who transforms decorating chaos into pleasing design for the bewildered homeowner, our God will step in and do the same for us. All we need to do is feed our grand plans to the shredder, relinquish control, trust Him unconditionally, subjugate our understanding to His, and in all areas of our lives, acknowledge His sovereignty and power. Then we will see our life's path made straight, our bewilderment vanished.

Question for reflection: Have you figured out yet that His way is the way and all you have to do is trust His design?

Legacy

"I have fought the good fight, I have finished the race, I have kept the faith."

2 Timothy 4:7

These words of Paul in his letter to Timothy declare the legacy the apostle leaves behind. They remind me that we all will leave a legacy of some kind one day. As Christians, we want our legacy to be one of faith rather than faithlessness. But if we are not careful and deliberate in how we live, we may look back as our journey nears its end and see a disturbing picture of fights not worthy of the conflict, forsaken races, and faltering faith. Just the opposite of what Paul was able to proclaim.

To be able to claim that we have fought the good fight means we will have engaged only in the battles God championed and led, not those we selected. Scripture teaches us that God's battles are not "against flesh and blood, but against the rulers, against authorities, against the power of the dark world and against the spiritual forces of evil in heavenly realms" (Ephesians 6:12). Simply put, these are the battles we fight to have minds of Christ in every aspect of our lives. For when our minds are stayed (focused) on God, we will be engaged in the fights He purposes for us.

To be able to claim that we have finished the race means we will have pressed on, not having grown weary and sat down on the curb side of life. We will not have taken detours or short cuts to reach the finish line. Rather we will have continued "toward the goal to win the prize for which God has called us." (Philippians 3:14)

To be able to claim that we have kept the faith means we will not have lost sight of our journey's purpose. In everything we will have sought to discern and to practice not our own, but God's will for our lives. Our keeping the faith will have been intentional, not cursory. As Christians, we have no option. A life of faith, not faithlessness, is what we are called to live and in so doing, leave as our legacy.

Question for reflection: What legacy will you leave?

Answers

...”Naked I came from my mother's womb, and naked I will depart. The Lord gave and the Lord has taken away; may the name of the Lord be praised.”
Job 1:20-21

Beginning in early childhood, we seek answers. The one word query "Why?" tests the patience of many a parent, childcare giver, and teacher. This answer quest shapes our formative years and follows us well into our senior season. No matter what, we want to know, "Why?"

The Book of Job challenges us on many levels. It is a story that speaks to many themes: suffering, patience, satanic attack, pride, trust, and the ultimate goodness of God. But perhaps its greatest challenge is its revelation that sometimes we don't receive an answer to our "Why?" Job suffers loss of possessions, family, and health; his friends fail to console him; his wife's advice flies in the face of his beliefs. And Job never receives an answer to why these calamities befall him.

How are we twenty first century Christians to experience life in light of Job's story? Are we to expect that the reason for our challenges and setbacks will be explained? When we're daily practicing our faith principles, should we be surprised when disaster strikes for no apparent reason? Do we expect divine explanation when we've done nothing to deserve it, but sorrow still wraps her heavy arms around us? The lesson of Job for us is hard. We've been socialized to expect answers. But as the story of Job illustrates, they will not always come. Sometimes the answer is simply our acceptance that there is no answer, no reason we can fathom. And like Job, we come to understand we may never know the "Why?", but if we continue to trust Him, we will always know the One who is sovereign. The One who knew us before we were conceived and who knows the beginning and end of our very existence. Knowing Him is enough.

Question for reflection: Do you still struggle to understand why things happen to you that you feel are undeserved or have you learned to accept that some things may never be known?

Jesus Peace

"Peace I leave with you; my peace I give you. I do not give to you as the world gives. Do not let your hearts be troubled and do not be afraid."

John 14:27

Today when we speak of "Peace", we typically make reference to efforts to stop conflicts in various places around the world. This peace is the state or condition politicians and other leaders seek to bring to opposing sides that are locked in combat both on battle fields and around conference tables. This peace represents external conditions arrived at only when, and if, those engaged in the struggle put aside their differences and agree to its terms. This kind of peace, as history illustrates, tends to be temporary, lasting only until the next incident flares and ignites the "conflict" gene once again.

By contrast, Scripture teaches us that Jesus offers a different peace. It is not the kind artificially imposed by treaties and rhetoric. Rather, the peace He gives is

His peace, unique in that only He can bestow it. It is a guardian peace that goes to the heart and soul of our being and calms us in a way that stops worry, anxiety, and fear at the threshold. Jesus' peace sinks deep and swallows up the conflicting factions of our day to day experiences. It allows us to deal with the ups and downs confident that where His peace is, there He is also. His words are simple, yet powerful. "Do not let your hearts be troubled," He says, "and do not be afraid." He can proclaim this to us because He has given us His peace and He knows that if we accept it as He freely gives it, we can face whatever challenges arise with a calm, confident, assured spirit of victory. Praise God. Alleluia.

Reflection question: Does your response to life's challenges demonstrate Christ's peace is embedded in you?

All for God's Glory

When he heard this, Jesus said, "This sickness will not end in death. No, it is for God's glory so that God's Son may be glorified through it.

John 11:4.

After I read the first seven verses of John, chapter eleven, I was drawn back to verse four. As the Scripture reads, Jesus receives word that His friend Lazarus is sick. We assume it was an urgent message, sort of like calling 911 today. Lazarus' family needed immediate help, so they called for their "paramedic" in the person of Jesus of Nazareth, the known healer and miracle worker. However, unlike today's paramedics who immediately take to the road, sirens screaming and lights flashing when calls for help reach them, Jesus delays his response by two days. Verse four tells us why and helps us understand God's sovereignty. Lazarus' illness and subsequent death were allowed to occur for God's glory to be manifested through Jesus' actions.

We understand that the God of Lazarus is the same God whose divine plans allow our trials and tests, including illnesses and death. We also accept that it is in these trials that God often acts in mysterious ways. Sometimes our answers are immediate; other times His response takes months or even years and in some instances never comes as we hope. We may not be called back to life as before, if we are called back at all. Yet we believe that whatever He allows to happen is deliberate, akin to Jesus' two day delay in going to Lazarus. The waiting for His arrival is the time He uses to bring us back into focus, to renew our basic beliefs, to strengthen our faith, to allow us to surrender totally to His will. And when He does respond, there is no doubt to whom the glory belongs. God and God alone!

Question for reflection: Do you glorify God regardless of His response to your needs?

No, in all these things we are more than conquerors
Through him who loved us,
For I am convinced that neither death nor life,
Neither angels nor demons,
Neither the present nor the future, nor any powers,
Neither height nor depth,
Nor anything else in all creation,
Will be able to separate us from the love of God
That is in Christ Jesus our Lord.

Romans 8:37-39

Forever Relevant

"Now fear the Lord and serve him with all faithfulness. Throw away the gods your forefathers worshiped…and serve the Lord. But if serving the Lord seems undesirable to you, then choose for yourselves whom you will serve.…But as for me and my household, we will serve the Lord."

Joshua 24:14-15

One of the things I love most about the Bible is how relevant the stories and experiences of God's people are to us who live more than two thousand years later. Logically you would think there would be little to commend this Word of God to us. The world is vastly different than when Joshua and the Israelites settled in the land promised to them. Yet reading Joshua's words to his people illustrates that this Holy Book brings truth irrespective of the century.

When we accept Christ as our personal Savior, we are called to throw away those things we worshiped before - material possessions, titles, and prestige - and worship only Him faithfully. This is exactly what Joshua calls the Hebrews to do - to throw away the stuff they felt important before the Lord delivered them. Notice that God does not force Himself upon us however. Christ bids us to come unto Him, but leaves the acceptance of the invitation to our free will. At this juncture of their faith journey, the Israelites too have a choice. If serving God seemed undesirable to them, they were free to choose for themselves whom they would serve.

Joshua declares his intentions clearly with his words in verse fifteen; we Christians do the same when we accept that Christ's death on the cross was for our salvation. In turn we follow His example by our life style choices confident that faithfulness in our choosing leads to the "promised land" of eternal life. With the Israelites we say, "We will serve the Lord because He is our God."

You'll never convince me that this great, holy book, the Bible, is not meant for us today and for generations yet to come. Praise God for his Word.

Question for reflection: What Bible stories inspire you daily to "serve the Lord"?

Immediately

"Come, follow me," Jesus said, "and I will make you fishers of men." At once they left their nets and followed him. Going on from there, he saw two other brothers.... They were in a boat with their father preparing their nets. Jesus called them, and immediately they left the boat and their father and followed him.

Matthew 4: 18-22

Consider the scene. Two sets of brothers, Simon Peter and Andrew, James and John are up early, already engaged in the routines of their work: preparing nets and casting them to catch fish. Jesus walks by. Scripture does not tell us, but we assume He had passed others who were also fishing or preparing to fish. For whatever reason He stops at these two spots along the Galilean Sea shore and calls to these particular men. Without hesitation, they cease their work, ask no questions, and follow the Master's call. Wow! Had they heard of Jesus already - this new itinerant preacher exhorting people to repent of their sins? Were they just waiting, hoping he would pass their way so that they could join up with him? We don't know what stirred the brothers' response. What we do know is Jesus issued them an invitation and their RSVP was immediate. What trust, what faith, what hope these first followers demonstrated when they responded to that call. Just like us today, right?

Let's leave the Galilean Sea shore and travel two thousand years plus to the places we live and work. Consider the contemporary scene of Sunday morning worship services. The invitation to follow Jesus goes out as the Lord again passes by in the spoken word and song. Unlike the scene at Galilee however, the response to the call is often not immediate, if it comes at all. Many who hear the call think the time is not right. They reason that their living is already jam-packed with responsibilities: career, children, family, community, and social obligations. Impossible to lay down the "nets" and follow now, maybe later.

Alas. Even with our advanced knowledge, we modern day folk fail to grasp what the early hearers of the call understood. No matter the season of our lives, when Jesus calls, we lay aside anything that encumbers or delays us and follow him. Notice that the four brothers in our Scripture did not try to take their nets with them. These tools would have been an unnecessary burden. Neither did they say to Jesus, "Give me a while to get my family situated. Then I will join you." Their spirits let them know that this call could not wait. They needed to act then to claim the life Jesus offered.

Like these first followers, we must not hesitate, procrastinate, or deliberate when Jesus calls, "Follow me." With complete trust and faith in Him, we must immediately lay aside the things of the world that tempt or ensnare us. The call cannot wait. It is urgent. The time for obedience is immediate; it is now.

Question for reflection: Does your living demonstrate that nothing is standing in the way of your "yes" to Jesus' call?

Worship God!

At this I fell at his feet to worship him. But he said to me, "Do not do it! I am a fellow servant with you and your brothers who hold to the testimony of Jesus. Worship God!…"

Revelation 19:10

The biblical passage for the day was the nineteenth chapter of the Book of Revelation. When I got to the tenth verse, the words seemed to jump off the page: "Worship God!" Emphatically, the angel at whose feet John fell, swiftly halted the apostle's faulty worship with his imperative, "Do not do it!" The apostle had allowed himself to become so caught up in the splendor of the revelations opened to him that he was about to worship the wrong being. The angel, though heavenly, was not God!

As Christians, we are wise to remember this encounter. Often in our contemporary culture, we are blinded by the charisma, the magnetism, and the dynamic personality of some church leaders. Lacking in spiritual discernment, we elevate them to God-like status, forgetting that they are our fellow servants. And soon enough we find ourselves paying homage to them rather than to the God we both serve.

Similarly, we modern day saints have to guard against the tendency to worship the novelties, rituals, traditions, and technological trends of our faith expression. Too readily we embrace these ever changing styles and in the process allow them to influence us away from worship of God. As the angel cautioned John, our worship is to be Christ-centered. We fall at the feet of no ministry, no person, no title, no denomination, and no latest innovation for a "true worship experience". God and God alone is worthy of our worship and praise. All else fades before His glory.

Question for reflection: Are you worshipping God or the trappings that surround him?

God's Time

But I trust in you, O Lord; I say, "You are my God."
My times are in your hands; deliver me from my
enemies and from those who pursue me.

Psalms 31:14-15

In I Samuel 26: 1-12, David comes upon his enemy King Saul asleep in camp and quite an easy prey for anyone seeking to harm him. David, however, refuses to take advantage of this opportunity for vengeance. His conversation with his aide who wants to strike the king dead reveals David understands that God's time supersedes our time. He says, "As surely as the Lord lives… the Lord himself will strike him."

He did not struggle, as we often do, to give the situation over to God and wait on Him to move. David understood better than we that the battle was not his, but the Lord's. We could save ourselves many frustrations and anxieties by imitating David's approach. More importantly, if we master God's command to us to "Be still and know that I am God" (Psalm 46:10), we will see our lives unfold in ways ordained by the Master. We permit God's time to set the pace and determine the end. We resist the urge or even the opportunity to "fix" the problem unless the Holy Spirit reveals to us that "This is the way. Walk in it." (Isaiah 30:21).

Question for reflection: How do you understand the concept of "God's time"?

Slowing Time

My times are in your hands….

Psalm 31:15

It's so fast - this passage of time. We celebrate the start of a new year bundled in warm coats and caps, but before we can slip out of our gloves, the swim suit edition of *Sports Illustrated* stares at us from the newsstand.   Life speeds at such a pace that we often feel disoriented by the quickness of it. Most days end being too short for all we want and think we need to do in them. We wonder if it is age that gives us this perspective or our growing awareness of God's purposes being played out in His creation.

The innocence of childhood, when time seemed to move in slow motion, is long gone, replaced by a speeding train of hours that escapes us. Experiences piled high as laundry left undone for several weeks erode naiveté and replace it with the harsh realities of living. Yet as we draw closer to our Creator and struggle to live as He wills rather than as we want, we discover our perception of not having enough time is caused by our efforts to do both God's will and our own. When we live that way, we run out of time everyday because the day is finite. I imagine that we will find that the more we drop our will from the day's agenda and concentrate on God's will, our days will not lack enough hours. We will have more than enough time to accomplish what truly needs doing. The time will slow to God's pace and not ours. It's certainly worth a try.

Question for reflection: What controls your agenda – God's To Do List or your own?

Heavenly Directions

Show me your ways, O Lord, teach me your paths;
guide me in your truth and teach me, for you are God
my Savior, and my hope is in you all day long.
                                          Psalm 25:4-5

A recent need to find directions to a downtown restaurant sent me to my computer. Like many internet users, I am a faithful fan of "Map Quest", a popular web site resource. Following the necessary data input, the system delivers route information, providing not only a map, but also text directions. With access to a computer, it's a certainty that you can find your way to wherever you want to go.

As I waited for the directions to print, I reflected upon how like the "Map Quest" is our Lord's Word, the Bible. In truth, we can consider it our spiritual map quest, the resource to which we turn when we need "divine directions." When we are tempted to go our own way, to choose the world rather than the Word, the psalmist reminds us that the Lord leads us beside still waters, restores us, guides us in right paths, and even leads us safely through the shadow of death (Psalm 23). When we humble ourselves before the Lord, the Bible tells us that He will guide us in what is right and teach us His way (Psalm 25:9). When we seek absolute assurance of His faithfulness to lead us, the Bible proclaims "For this God is our God for ever and ever; he will be our guide even to the end." (Psalm 48:14). The Bible assures us that His hand always guides us no matter where we are (Psalm 139:7-10); that it guides us in the way of wisdom and leads us along straight paths (Proverbs 4:11); that the Lord will guide us always and satisfy our needs (Isaiah 58:11).

God's "map quest", His Holy Word, is the only directional resource Christians need to reach their ultimate destination. As I lifted the directions to the restaurant from the printer tray, I realized that if I follow my Lord's directions as revealed in the Bible as carefully as I do the ones I get online, then I am sure to reach my divine destination-eternal life with my Father.

Question for reflection: Are you lost and still searching or have you tapped into the divine resource that will lead you home?

Priorities

"…The Lord, the God of heaven, has given me all the kingdoms of the earth and he has appointed me to build a temple for him at Jerusalem in Judah. Anyone of his people among you-may his God be with him, and let him go up to Jerusalem in Judah and build the temple of the Lord, the God of Israel…" Then the heads of Judah and Benjamin, and the priests and Levites-everyone whose heart God had moved-prepared to go up and build the house of the Lord in Jerusalem.

Ezra 1:2-5

During a devotional time, I was reminded once again how the Bible is indeed a lamp for our feet and a light for our paths (Psalm 119:105). The more diligently we read and meditate upon it, the more direction it provides for our daily living. I was reading a passage in Ezra, an unheralded, but nonetheless key priest and leader of the Jewish people during the period of their return to Jerusalem following the exile to Babylon. In his book, he chronicles the Jews' efforts to rebuild God's house, their temple. It seemed the rebuilding of the temple was far more important to them than even the building of security walls around the city. The commentary writer's observation that the people understood two things - a stone wall was no protection if they didn't have a right relationship with God and getting their spiritual lives in order was more important than national security concerns - struck a cord with me. I immediately thought of how applicable this piece of biblical history is to Christians today.

We who profess the Christian faith would do well to heed the implications of the actions of the returning exiles. All too often in our understanding of what we need to do to build successful lives, we concentrate our efforts in establishing external structures: degree, career, marriage, possessions, children, and financial security. Constructing these "walls" ranks at the top of our priority list. But when we subjugate the building of our spiritual lives to these structures, we exist on unstable ground. Our foundation is not secured in the Lord, but in the unpredictable, unreliable hands of man. The Jewish exiles who returned show us a better way.

At each significant juncture of our life's building blocks - educational decisions, career choices, marital and family planning, material acquisitions, or financial decisions- our first efforts should be to make sure our plans and desires are in accord with God's will and purposes. We do this by staying connected to Him through prayer, worship, and knowledge of His Word. We are intentional in our building to seek first His kingdom. We ask for His guidance. We seek the leading of His Spirit. When we follow this path to right relationship with Him, we order our priorities, as did our religious ancestors. Like them, we secure our spiritual temples first, confident that when the time comes to build the external walls, God will be with us.

Question for reflection: Is your relationship with God truly your first priority?

Remembering the Blessings

The people served the Lord throughout the lifetime of Joshua and of the elders who outlived him and who had seen all the great things the Lord had done for Israel. ...After that whole generation had been gathered to their fathers, another generation grew up, who knew neither the Lord nor what he had done for Israel. Then the Israelites did evil in the eyes of the Lord and served the Baals. They forsook the Lord, the God of their fathers, who had brought them out of Egypt.

Judges 2:7-12

You may remember the story. Joshua dismisses the Israelites to go and take possession of the land God promised to them and throughout the remainder of Joshua's lifetime and that of the elders, the people served the Lord. Something happened, however, after the generation that had personally known the Lord's blessings passed away. The succeeding generation "neither knew the Lord nor what He had done for Israel." As I reflected upon this Scripture, I wondered why the succeeding generation did not know of the Lord and what He had done for them. After all in at least two recorded instances, Moses had instructed the people to teach their children and the children after them what they had seen God do (Deuteronomy 4:9). Again in Deuteronomy 11:19, Moses reminded the Israelites to teach the children, to talk to them at home, when they were out and about and when they lay down and arose to worship. It seems logical that if the Israelites had done this, had continued to pass the stories of the blessings and faithfulness of God, the generation following Joshua and the elders would have indeed known the Lord and worshipped Him only. But they did not. Why? Perhaps for the same reasons that the generations that followed Jesus' time on earth did not, despite His parting command to them to go out and teach others what he had taught them (Matthew 28:20).

Our Christian ancestors, like the Israelites, got so busy with their living that they forgot their life source! If we look back at our Christian history in the early years as the church got established, we see those who had experienced Christ's miracles and teachings first or second hand continuing to worship God alone. Even in later years as the church maintained its prominence as the center of the community, the people passed what they had been taught to their children and grandchildren. In time though the business of life claimed precedence over the Creator of life and gradually the people let slip through frantic fingers the witness of and obedience to their faith. What God commanded the Israelites, what Christ commanded us became the stuff of "old folks" and "old school", out of sync with contemporary living and thinking. Now many of us stand just where that generation after Joshua and the elders stood - not knowing God and what He has done for us, separated from Him, worshipping our "Baals".

Yet, as He did with our biblical ancestors, our ever-faithful Father does with us. He waits for our return to Him, to remember His blessings, His mercy and His grace. And in that remembering, He calls us to teach those who will become our next generation. The responsibility for the passing of our faith rests with all who claim His name. Who will our children and grandchildren worship? The Baals of their age because we failed to teach them, or the eternal God of our Christian faith.

Question for reflection: What are you doing to help those who will come after you remember the blessings of our Lord?

Living Water –
Broken Cisterns

"Has a nation ever changed its gods? (Yet they are not gods at all.) But my people have exchanged their Glory for worthless idols. Be appalled at this, O heavens, and shudder with great horror," declares the Lord. "My people have committed two sins: They have forsaken me, the spring of living water, and have dug their own cisterns, broken cisterns that cannot hold water."

Jeremiah 2:11-13

This text of Jeremiah reminds us that if we aren't careful, we can find ourselves in the same condition as that of the Israelites to whom the Lord addresses these words in the book of Jeremiah. Unless discerning, we may replace the one true God for our contemporary gods of money, fame, position, prestige, possessions, and favor. As in Jeremiah's time, none of these gods is capable of giving us what God alone offers us _ living water that guarantees eternal life. When in our self sufficiency we turn our backs on Him, and seek to build our security and future with things that will not last; we are in effect doing what the Israelites did - digging our own cisterns.

How then do we who are traveling the road to eternity insure that we do not exchange God's living water for the very things that signal success and good fortune in our time? First, we ask ourselves a simple question. "Does this decision or desire honor God or me?" If what you're getting ready to pursue does not include opportunities for you to be guided by God's will instead of your own, it is probably one that honors you.

Secondly, we remember that we have nothing that God has not already ordained for us. This means we worship the giver of all good gifts, and not the gift or the possession itself. It has no value apart from the God who gave it. Finally, we intentionally seek only those attributes of God's living water that flow from His cistern: love, joy, peace, gentleness, kindness, goodness, faithfulness, patience, and self control. Nothing we construct can last or sustain us as this fruit of His Spirit (Galatians 5:22). Anything we build without Him will only disappear through the holes of our clay-formed cisterns.

Questions for reflection: Who's your construction foreman? Do your plans focus on the now or the eternal?

Is There Any Help?

When I said, "My foot is slipping," your love, O
Lord, supported me. When anxiety was great within
me, your consolation brought joy to my soul.

Psalm 94:18-19

As Christians, we are wise to recall that life's circumstances will test our faith for as long as our journey here continues. Our acceptance of and belief in Christ Jesus does not immunize us against the enemy's wiles or the challenges of living day in and day out. In fact, nowhere in the Gospels does Jesus promise that discipleship will be easy or trouble free. In Matthew, He proclaims clearly that His followers can expect persecution, insults, false and evil testimony against them (Matthew 5:10-11).

Often, we modern day followers of Christ experience less than ideal responses to our profession of faith. How many of us have been ostracized in the workplace because of our integrity or refusal to accommodate negative, secular mores? In our social settings, how often have we been labeled "naïve" or "simplistic" because we voiced a truth based upon God's Word? In our familial and friendship circles, how frequently do we find our beliefs being attacked as politically incorrect or out of sync with today's world?

Because we are human, "forgiven not perfect", we ask ourselves in these situations, "Can anyone help me get through this?" At these moments, we might reflect upon the words of the Psalmist. Indeed, God's unfailing love for us can restore us to upright positions of faith and trust. His love is more powerful than any attack that seeks to push us off our faith foundation. His words of comfort and assurance can console our heartache, calm our fear, quiet our anxiousness and bring us peace in our valleys and joy in our mornings.

No, our walk of faith was never intended to be the monotonous, predictable ride on the merry-go-round. Often it is more akin to the heart-thumping experience of a giant roller coaster. For it is in the turbulent twists and turns, the catch-your-breath ascents and the stomach-churning descents that we come to realize there is help. He stands at the exit of the turnstile as we breathlessly emerge, worn and weary. Hands outstretched, Our Savior says, "Come to me. I love you. I am all the help you need."

Question for reflection: When the challenges come, to whom do you turn for help?

Poster Person for Giving

Jesus sat down opposite the place where the offerings were put and watched the crowd putting their money into the temple treasury...a poor widow came and put in two very small copper coins, worth only a fraction of a penny...Jesus said, "I tell you the truth, this poor widow has put more into the treasury than all the others. They gave out of their wealth; but she, out of her poverty, put in everything - all she had to live on."

Mark 12:41-44

I have a dear sister friend who I think is a contemporary picture of the widow Jesus draws attention to in the Gospel of Mark. I call her a Poster Person for Giving. No, she isn't a widow and nor is she is poverty-stricken. However she is neither rich nor well off by today's standards and certainly does not possess the things of wealth. Yet, in her giving she reminds me of the widow because she gives out of whatever she has. She takes this discipline of giving farther than many think is necessary; she gives not only of her time; she gives of her possessions; she gives of herself to acknowledge the humanity of those who have less.

Long before most of us paid attention to the homeless on our streets, this sister-friend kept change in her car to give to whoever asked. When she crosses their path on neighborhood sidewalks, she doesn't just say "hello". She stops to talk and to listen. What's even more astounding is that she calls many of them by name. Often she goes into a store or restaurant to buy a meal for them on the spot. When cold weather comes, she goes to places where she knows the homeless squat to bring socks and blankets. Not long ago she grew her luxurious thick hair very long just to have it cut so that she could donate it to an organization that makes wigs for cancer patients.

Both the widow in Mark's Gospel and my sister-friend teach us that Jesus is pleased when we understand what He expects of us in our giving - sharing that with which He has blessed us in whatever ways we can, no matter our circumstances.

Question for reflection: How pleased is Jesus with your giving habits?

Praising Through

My praise is continually of you...And [I] will praise
you yet more and more.

Psalm 71:6, 14

As she lifted intercessory prayers this morning, my
prayer line co-worker used the phrase, "praise your way
through." The thought surfaced that learning to praise
our way through difficult circumstances is a spiritual
discipline worth acquiring. As Christians we know that
praise is our expression of joy to the Lord. We offer
"adoration praise" for who He is and "thanksgiving
praise" for what He does. Many of us will admit that
praising Him for what He does comes a lot easier than
offering Him praises for who He is. Expression of
adorations just doesn't seem to flow as easily. Perhaps
we tiptoe around adoration simply because we haven't
mastered "praising through."

Generally, we offer praises of thanksgiving when our
trials turn to triumphs. After months of job hunting, our

finances dwindling daily, the call comes. We join the world of the gainfully employed. Praises of thanksgiving go up. Or the diagnosis for mom is serious. We pace the corridor outside the surgical waiting room, worriedly praying, "Please, Lord. Heal momma." After what seems forever, the doctor emerges and with a smile announces, "She made it. She'll be fine." Praises of thanksgiving go up. Such praise is almost automatic. As I understood the prayer of my sister-in-Christ on the prayer line, we Christians are to be as fervent in our praises during our ordeals as we are after they end. Praises of adoration while in the throes of tribulation remind us who God is. He is our sovereign Lord, the majestic Creator of the earth and all that is in it. In the midst of our suffering, we adore Him with praises for His compassion. As we shuffle wearily through our hardships, we adore Him with praise for His faithfulness. We shower Him with our adoration because He alone is worthy of our praises. Learning to "praise through" is what we offer Him during the "good, the bad, and the ugly" in this grand adventure called life.

Question for reflection: The next time trouble strikes, will you be able to praise God both through it and after it?

Prayer, Not Panic

When Arioch, the commander of the king's guard, had gone out to put to death the wise men of Babylon, Daniel spoke to him with wisdom and tact. He asked the king's officer, "Why did the king issue such a harsh degree?" Arioch then explained the matter to Daniel. At this, Daniel went to the king and asked for time, so that he might interpret the dream for him. Then Daniel returned to his house and explained the matter to his friends...He urged them to plead for mercy from God...

Daniel 2:14-18

If ever there was a time for terror and panic, it was then. The king's edict was about to be executed. All wise men in the kingdom were to be killed. This included Daniel and his three friends, exiles from Judah who had entered the king's service as advisers after impressing him with their wisdom and understanding. Upon hearing the decree, Daniel's actions provide an excellent model for every believer on how to respond when life's challenges seem especially scary. And trust me, those frightening situations will appear at various times during the journey.

Daniel first clarifies his understanding of the problem. And he does it calmly, "with wisdom and tact." In other words, hysteria and rash actions are not his initial response to a crisis. When we can keep our emotions in check, we are more likely to see a problem with greater clarity. Daniel's behavior encourages us to approach our circumstances with a sense of order, not chaos.

Next Daniel goes to the source of the problem. Rather than push the panic button, with confidence bolstered by his experiences of God's faithfulness, he asks for what amounted to a reprieve. Similarly, before we go weak-kneed with panic, we are to remember how the Lord has brought us through in the past. Then we can seek solutions with assurance rather than timidity.

Finally, as did Daniel, we take our concerns to God not in panic, but in personal and collective prayer. We understand that the fervent prayers of fellow believers get God's attention. So, in concert with friends who believe in the power of prayer, we bring our petitions to Him, confident that no matter the seriousness or the urgency of the challenge, He will hear and answer us according to His will and purpose.

Question for reflection: When the news is unbelievably bad, what will be your first response - panic or prayer?

Prelude to Eternity

For God so loved the world that he gave his one and only son, that whoever believes in him shall not perish but have eternal life.

John 3:16

These words of God's promise as recorded by the Apostle John flow easily from the tongue of most Christian believers. One of the first Bible verses we memorize as children, it remains on deposit in our spiritual memory banks, available for easy withdrawal whenever the need arises. Typically, it is to this depository we go when our confidence is shaken, our spirits depleted, or our path obscured.

As Christians striving to live each day better than we lived the one before, we are challenged to understand the importance of this seemingly simple Scripture. We find that as it was from the onset of creation, God acts first. He loved. Can there be any greater boost to our sense of his purpose and will in our lives than the knowledge that God first loved us? Before we even came to be, he knew us and loved us. And as we see, it was not a passive, inert love. The Scripture is clear. He loved actively by giving his son asour pathway to divinity. Is there anything else capable of filling our spirit with such overwhelming joy than this gift of Jesus?

And what does the Holy lover and giver require of us in return? Only that we believe. For when we believe with every fiber of our being that Jesus is God's Son and our hope for salvation, the path clears. We see with unclouded eyes the road that will take us to eternity. We understand our final destiny is not the grave. No. We will not perish, because we believe. And just as God loved actively, we believe actively. Day to day we reveal our belief by the manner in which we live in the world. We are intentional in our demonstration that Jesus is our Savior. We embrace the promise of John 3:16 and our role in its manifestation as the gateway to eternity.

Question for reflection: Where are you in your understanding of God's promise and your response to it?

Privileged Perspective

Then Jesus turned to his disciples and said privately, "Blessed are the eyes that see what you see. For I tell you that many prophets and kings wanted to see what you see but did not see it, and to hear what you hear but did not hear it."

Luke 10:23-24

The Scriptures do not tell us the reaction of Jesus' disciples to these words He spoke privately to them. We can only wonder if they truly appreciated their unique position. In the Old Testament, God had spoken through the prophets of the promised Messiah, but they did not get to actually see and hear Him in the flesh. These contemporaries of Jesus, the ones He chose to follow Him, were blessed indeed that they were able to witness firsthand the fulfillment of Scripture, to be a physical part of Jesus' time on earth. By their actions during His ministry however, we can conclude that the disciples were slow to recognize the privilege of their position. Not until His appearances to them following His resurrection did they finally understand the authenticity of His claims. We can only speculate how Jesus' ministry might have been different if His disciples had truly listened and understood from the beginning.

We twenty first century Christians can claim also a unique position. With over 2000 years of church history, the Bible in various translations, and countless witnesses to Christ's power, ours is a privileged perspective. No, we don't walk in the physical with Him, but we do walk with the comfort of the Holy Spirit, the comforter God sent to be with us when Christ returned to His Father. The Spirit resides in our hearts and minds and encourages us in our faith journey. His living Word, the Bible, equips us for the work of kingdom building as He commissioned at His ascension. His teachers and preachers inspire and shepherd our evangelical efforts.

With this perspective of time, we are blessed with the necessary knowledge to represent Christ Jesus without hesitancy or reluctance. This privileged position gives us all we need to follow Him, assured of the outcome of our obedience. His ministry continues and thrives through our daily actions. We do not lightly wear the mantle of our faith, but rather seek every opportunity to shoulder the responsibility that comes with this privileged perspective.

Question for reflection: How do you identify with this concept of "privileged perspective"?

Promises

I call with all my heart; answer me, O Lord, and I will obey your decrees.

Psalm 119:145

Oh, the vows and promises we make to God when we are in trouble, facing some crisis or tragedy! "Lord, if you just help me now. Lord, if you just take away this burden, I will never do that again. I'll start back to church. I'll call my mother. I'll stop drinking." The promises of what we will do if only God will deliver us go on and on. We are not unique. Our faith ancestors, the Israelites were just like us. "I will come to your temple with burnt offerings and fulfill my vows to you - vows my lips promised and my mouth spoke when I was in trouble" (Psalm 66:13-14). The psalmist could be you or me.

At the moment we utter the vows or promises, we are sincere because we recognize from whence our help comes: the Lord God. Our problem is the same as it was for the Israelites; all too soon after God has indeed answered our cries, the crisis or trouble has passed, and we have returned to our normal routines and circumstances, we forget what we promised God we would do if he delivered us. Despite His faithfulness to us, we are not faithful to Him. When we think we have everything under control, we somehow forget that it was His hand that brought us through.

We thank God however, because we serve a Savior who is not only faithful when we are not, but who is always ready to offer us grace upon grace, over and over again. Instead of turning from us, He turns toward us, forgiving, beckoning, rescuing, and seeking to reconcile us to Himself.

Reflection question: How can you avoid the trap of forgetting what you promised God when your life challenges have been resolved?

Pruning the Faithful

*"I am the true vine, and my Father is the gardener.
He cuts off every branch in me that bears no fruit,
while every branch that does bear fruit he prunes so
that it will be even more fruitful.*
John 15:1-2

My husband is the acknowledged gardener of the family. His "green thumb" produces dazzling displays of colorful flowers each year as he carefully tends the blooms in our flowerbeds and borders. With the discernment of a gardener's eye, he moves amidst the blossoms, clipping away dead blooms and leaves. This cutting is necessary, he says, to promote the plants' continuing growth. If he leaves the dead flowers on the plants, they drain nutrients from the roots and the plant's blooming potential is stunted.

As followers of Christ, we understand from this "vine and branches" lesson Jesus taught His disciples that God does pretty much the same thing with us as my husband does with his plants, and for the same reason. Christ is the vine; God is the gardener. We are the branches that God carefully tends to insure that the vine's growth - the building of God's kingdom - continues.

Sometimes though, we branches fall away from the practice of our faith and revert to old, destructive habits. We become like useless, dried up branches. We cease producing the fruit of the Spirit and witnessing to God's glory. To avoid damage to His Kingdom's growth, our gardener, God, may have to prune some of the useless branches, just as does my husband.

At the same, God encourages those who are faithful branches to become even more fruitful. With the gardener's discerning eye and disciplined hand, He prunes these branches so that they produce more good works for the Kingdom. Sometimes the pruning may hurt; what cut doesn't? But it is in the disciplining through trials and tests that God grows our faith and character, the ingredients we need as branches to be fruitful. Like the flowers bursting with vibrancy under my husband's care, the fruitful branches of God's vineyard yield a hundred-fold as their labor bears witness to the Lord's glory.

Question for reflection: What fruit are you producing as a branch of Christ?

Rebellion – Then and Now

When I have brought them into the land flowing with milk and honey, the land I promised on oath to their forefathers, and when they eat their fill and thrive, they will turn to other gods and worship them, rejecting me and breaking my covenant.

Deuteronomy 31:20

The Israelites stand at the brink of the Promised Land, ready finally to claim God's promise to their ancestors. Imagine their weariness of body and their eagerness of soul after so many years wandering in the desert to settle down and enjoy this land of "milk and honey." But God knew their future. He knew that soon their comfort and prosperity in this Promised Land would cause them to sin. They would break the covenant and embrace the gods of the land thus setting in motion a spiral of "disasters and difficulties" from which they would never totally recover.

As we study Old Testament Scripture, we 21st century Christians wonder how these chosen people could so easily forget God's saving grace and mercy, how they could turn their backs on the one who had delivered them time and time again. We shake our heads at their faithlessness. At such times of judgment, we often miss something crucial. Are we really so different than they? Do not our actions frequently mirror theirs?

Think back to the moment when you heard God's call and tearfully, with gratitude, said, "Yes. I will follow Jesus." You accepted his gift of forgiveness and salvation and began your new life in the land of "grace and mercy." All too soon though, after you had eaten your fill of his goodness, the other gods of the land crept back into those places you vowed to reserve for God. Book club selections gradually replaced Bible study. Prayer time became no time because mornings were too hectic and evenings too exhausting. Regular, consistent worship fell away to "I'll get there on Communion Sunday. Don't have the time to go every Sunday like I used to." Praise time became relegated to humming along with the CD on your way to sorority meeting or lunch with the girls.

And like the Israelites, as a result of turning our backs on God, we suffer many disasters and difficulties for our unfaithfulness. Yet, out of His abiding love, God continues to provide a way for us as He did for the Israelites, a way back to Him. He remembers that His son willingly paid the price for our continuing transgressions and stands even now just beyond the horizon waiting for us. Jesus Christ has prepared the place for us in the land of eternal life. It is there, awaiting our claim upon His promise.

Question for reflection: How much of your faith journey mirrors that of the Israelites?

Representing God

We are therefore Christ's ambassadors, as though
God were making his appeal through us.
I Corinthians 5:20

Society abounds with individuals "representing"
their affiliations with particular groups or organizations.
Greek sororities and fraternities. Professional and
collegiate sport teams. Military units. Street gangs. All
represent their group with colors, emblems, and other
paraphernalia that identify who they are. These external
accoutrements set them apart and help them make their
appeal to others.

The Apostle Paul's letter to the church at Corinth
reminds Christians that ours is a unique affiliation.
We represent God. Just as a secular ambassador is an
authorized resident representative or messenger of his
government, the residents of Christ's kingdom serve
as His divinely authorized ambassadors. We are the

medium through which His appeal reaches those searching for spiritual affiliation.

The challenge for Christian ambassadors is understanding exactly how we represent God in ways that aid His appeal. Just as the secular ambassador acknowledges the sovereignty of his government, Christian ambassadors must claim God as sovereign Lord of their lives. We do this by giving Him the glory for our successes and praising Him amidst our trials and challenges. Even when under attack, we remember whom we represent. Our responses and reactions will illuminate the depth of our faith.

As Christian ambassadors we stand firm in our belief that God will never abandon us. We become Daniel-like in our refusal to compromise our beliefs. Our badges of faith, trust, hope and love glow with the anointing of His Spirit. They allow His appeal to touch the heart of the outcast, the nonbeliever, the sick, and the tormented. Like the secular ambassador who delivers his government's message, God's ambassadors, with their internal accoutrements and outward displays of their faith, carry Christ's invitation of repentance, forgiveness, and salvation to all who would hear.

Question for reflection: Does your lifestyle represent God?

Resisting the Wonder

He said to them: "It is not for you to know the times or dates the Father has set by his own authority"… After he said this, he was taken up before their very eyes, and a cloud hid him from their sight. They were looking intently up into the sky as he was going, when suddenly two men dressed in white stood beside them. "Men of Galilee," they said, "why do you stand here looking into the sky? This same Jesus, who has been taken from you into heaven, will come back in the same way you have seen him go into heaven.

Acts 1:7-11

How wondrous it is to sit and contemplate Christ's return to earth from heaven. The thought of it fills any believer with pure joy! In fact the thought of it makes us just want to do nothing except sit and gaze toward heaven and speculate how it will be when He breaks through the barrier called Sky. Yet, I am reminded that believers can not "stop to stare" forever because we are called to live accountably while we wait. The luxury of "Stopping by the Woods…"is not one afforded to Disciples of Jesus Christ. We have as the poet Robert Frost writes, "promises to keep and miles to go before we sleep." In other words, our work of sharing the good news of the gospel, of tending the least, the lost, and the last, of living not for ourselves but for God's kingdom must go on even as we wait.

Our prayer is that every day, whenever we are tempted to just stop working and simply wait for His return, that the Lord will stir us back to His purpose for our lives_ service to others and witness to His salvation.

Question for reflection: Scripture tells us to "wait on the Lord." Does that mean to you that it is okay to spend your time "waiting for His return" as opposed to doing His work?

Risk and Release

Trust in the Lord with all your heart and lean not on your own understanding...Do not be wise in your own eyes.

Proverbs 3: 5, 7

Christians, who have "arrived", whether that success is manifested in their careers, income, martial bliss, parenthood, or countless possessions, are still often missing the key that fully opens the door to God's kingdom. For many, their effort to achieve their success is the very reason why they find it so difficult to allow God to take the lead in their lives. Outwardly, they wear well the robe of Christianity: Sunday morning services, deacon board member, choir soloist, and tither. What hinders their full experience of all God desires to give those who worship Him is their difficulty trusting God totally and risking what they have so carefully constructed over many years: their reliance on self.

Yes, reading the Sunday morning litanies, singing the comforting hymns, and bowing in prayer are easy enough. But being able to move beyond the cursory to a deeper relationship with God, of trusting Him to actually deliver a loved one from an addictive behavior, or a wayward child from self-destruction, or a parent from declining mental health, now that's a different story. After all, they didn't attain their status or influence by sitting on the sidelines. They worked for what they have and in the process learned to depend upon themselves to handle whatever came down the pike. After all, that religion stuff is okay, but it really can only go so far.

Yet, even as they (and yes, we) assume the posture of self-reliance, there is still no lasting peace. Something deep down inside our core chips at that wall of self-sufficiency. Under the Lord's direction, the Holy Spirit is relentless in hammering it down. God wants us; He alone has what we need - a peace that surpasses all understanding no matter the circumstances. All He requires of us is a release of our will and a heart willing to risk that He knows best our destiny. It is in that total surrender to Him that we gain the key to His eternal kingdom.

Question for reflection: Are you still in charge or have you released it to the Lord, risking all with Him?

Servant Greatness

...Whoever wants to be great among you must be your servant...just as the Son of Man did not come to be served, but to serve...

Matthew 20:26-28

Your attitude should be the same as that of Christ Jesus...taking the very nature of a servant...

Philippians 2:5-7

Why is Jesus' concept of servant hood so challenging for believers? Perhaps, because like our faith ancestors, we prefer to think of our Lord more as a conqueror than a servant. Someone named in the lead headline on the front page rather than mentioned in one or two lines in the Metro section. Despite Jesus' teachings in the Matthew passage and Paul's in his letter to the church at Philippi, it's easier for us to follow a "General Jesus" resplendent in the accepted accoutrements of greatness-power, prestige, possession, acclaim - than it is to be led by someone who shuns the perks of greatness for the undeniable sacrifices of the trenches.

I wondered about this disconnect between Jesus' words and our faith practice as I read from a devotional book. The idea that a life spent in service to others requires a mindset convinced of the value of such a life gave me tremendous pause. On the surface, Jesus' attitude toward servanthood and greatness seems simple enough. But to internalize this teaching to the point of practice is not easy. Who among us after all does not still delight in the three P's of greatness: privilege, power, and perks? When we perform an act of service, we expect recognition for our deed. When we give a sizable donation to a worthy cause, we expect our names to be prominent in the souvenir booklet or noted by those with influence and power. When we help feed the down trodden at the homeless shelter, we expect acknowledgement for the sacrifice of our time.

Oh, the gulf between what we profess and what we practice. Only total and absolute surrender of ourselves to God's purposes will enable us to close this gap. How else can we strip away the natural inclination to "be served" even in the midst of our serving? Our constant prayer must be for minds that embrace Jesus' concept of "servanthood" and reject the human tendency toward self and its exaltation. Help us, Lord. We need you.

Question for reflection: How hard is it for you to live the servanthood teachings of Jesus?

Seventy Times Seven

Then Peter came to Jesus and asked, "Lord, how many times shall I forgive my brother when he sins against me? Up to seven times?" Jesus answered, "I tell you, not seven times, but seventy times seven."
                                                                Matthew 18:21

After Jesus succinctly answered Peter's question as noted above, He continued His teaching with the parable of an unmerciful servant who, after being forgiven of his own debts, refused forgiveness to another servant who owed him. Outraged onlookers informed the master who promptly revoked his forgiveness and ordered the unmerciful servant jailed until he paid his debts. Jesus ends the parable with the warning that this is how our heavenly Father will treat us if we do not forgive others.

Recently, a loved one's outburst in which he expressed lingering anger over perceived wrongs done to him by family members reminded me of how difficult it is to adhere to Jesus' teachings about forgiveness. Even though like Peter, we are believers in Christ, we still struggle with the concept of forgiveness as He did. I can recall my own challenges in past years of letting go of the betrayals and pain loved ones caused. It was not easy. The human in us demands an accounting when we feel wronged. Yet experience teaches that the longer we hold onto the slight, the ill-spoken word, the contemptuous gesture, the rude remark, the betrayal of trust, the more difficult it becomes for us to forgive. We rationalize our behavior and justify our attitudes because we were the ones treated shabbily.

As Christians we must remember that the inability to forgive provides the devil a foothold. And with that foothold, he secures a position of influence. Once established, that influence feeds the wounds of betrayal or injustice or wrongdoing. It magnifies and becomes a stumbling block that restricts our own access to forgiveness. We then easily embrace the "I can forgive, but I can't forget" theology of forgiveness. When an incident provokes us, we readily recall past wrongs we suffered. Jesus' teaching demands both forgiveness and forgetfulness, or at least on-demand amnesia if bitterness accompanies the memory.

Only when we come to fully understand that God's Word is truth, that what He speaks is what He means, that Jesus' teachings are not options, but mandates for righteous living, are we able to be "doers" of His word. It's that simple. He tells us to forgive others as we ourselves are forgiven. He reminds us to be kind and compassionate to one another, forgiving each other just as Christ has forgiven us. So how often do we forgive?

As often as He forgives us. Jesus' teaching in Matthew 6:12 is crystal clear. "Forgive us our debts, as we also have forgiven our debtors."

Question for reflection: What past wrongs still govern your relationship with others? What must you do to truly forgive and forget them?

Soaring

…but those who hope in the Lord will renew their strength. They will soar on wings like eagles; they will run and not grow weary; they will walk and not faint.

Isaiah 40:31

During a recent morning walk around the neighborhood, I noticed several birds soaring in the blue-sky overhead. For several minutes, I kept my eyes focused on them as they swept smoothly over the rooftops. I recall wondering how it must feel to be able to glide like that so effortlessly, no fear of falling, no gravity pulling you downward to earth. What freedom, what power, and what strength the birds projected.

I understand why the prophet Isaiah used the imagery of a soaring eagle to describe a God who is everlasting and will always meet us at our points of need. Like the birds that fly without fear of falling, all we who believe in God must do is place our hope in Him, secure in the knowledge of His Omnipotence. When we surrender our doubts and fears to His power, when our faith and trust in His Word reaches higher and more exalted levels, He restores our physical and spiritual feebleness. He gives us the power I witnessed in the soaring birds, to glide above the trials and challenges of daily living, experiencing these imposters without being consumed by them.

When our hope rests in His promises, we run our earthly races with sure strides, confident of crossing the initial, mid-course, and final finishing lines. Not unlike Moses with his strength in tact at age 120 (Deuteronomy 34:7). When our hope rests in His Word, we journey upright, traversing the years allotted to us with bold witness, binding timidity and rejecting faintheartedness. When our hope is in the Lord, we live in strength and power.

Question for reflection: Are you soaring on faith like an eagle or still earthbound, flapping your wings like a chicken in the barnyard?

Someone Else's Challenges

Now faith is being sure of what we hope for and certain of what we do not see.

Hebrews 11:1

Often it is in someone else's challenge that we witness their faith at work to a degree that amazes and changes us. Remember the story of Daniel in the lion's den. His refusal to obey the king's edict landed him there even though the king favored him and despaired of having to carry out the punishment he himself had declared. Despite his apparent doom, never did Daniel waver in his beliefs or faith in God. As a result of his strong faith and miraculous deliverance, the king ordered all in his kingdom to worship Daniel's God.

The faith Daniel quietly exuded during his time of trial is the same faith I am witnessing currently in our son's challenge of securing permanent employment. Despite several starts and stops, bumps and hurdles, financial stressors and continuing family responsibilities, he has remained constant in his faith. Yes, he questions, searches and seeks to understand the "why" of his current circumstances, but he has not thrown in the towel and said, "Lord, I quit. You haven't delivered as you promised so I'm not going to trust you anymore." His faith that God will provide in due time keeps him going and sustains him when doubts creep in. Neither is he a stranger to the concept of the power of prayer as evidence of his faith. He continues to pray for himself and to ask for intercessory prayer.

Considering his relative youth, I am amazed at the degree of his perseverance and determination in finding the career choice God has for him. More importantly, like the king in Daniel's story, my son's trust in God changes me. His doggedness has caused me to be even more mindful that I am not to pay lip service to my faith. Watching and listening to him, I truly believe God will handle his challenges. Each day I am learning more and more to lean on God's promises and not my own understanding. I believe in the miracle of deliverance for my son as God leads him out of the unemployment den into the door of opportunity prepared for him. His response to his challenges has indeed strengthened my faith.

Question for reflection: Who has inspired you to greater faith by their handling of life's challenges?

Soufflé or Pudding

…Your enemy the devil prowls around like a roaring lion looking for someone to devour. Resist him, standing firm in the faith….

1 Peter 5:8-9

In his mini sermon, the minister's phrase," Soufflé American Religion," drew a few chuckles. Though he did not expound upon them, the phrase resonated with me as I scribbled them on my program. A few days later, the words came back to mind. I wondered what message the minister might have preached to explain them. "Soufflé American Religion". At first thought, the image of a perfectly puffed soufflé and Christian religion seem incongruent. The longer I held the image however, the clearer I saw the connection between them. A soufflé is light, full of air, and if slightly touched or poked will quickly deflate. Even as it bakes, the cook must be careful to do nothing that might cause it to fall. How like some of us who profess the Christian faith! By outward appearances we are puffed to perfection, seemingly in firm step with the tenets of our faith: Sunday worship, some form of service (choir, ushers, youth workers), Wednesday night Bible study. But, like the puffy soufflé that deflates at the slightest pressure, we "Soufflé Christians" too often cave in when the inevitable trials and tribulations touch our lives. Because our faith system is composed of the air of external rituals and doctrine rather than internal unwavering trust and faith in God's power, we easily lose heart and sink beneath the pokes of life's negative experiences.

Christ calls His followers to be more like pudding than soufflé in the practice of their faith. A "Pudding Christian" is soft in texture, yet firm in consistency, unaltered or damaged by touching and poking. The Pudding Christian requires no delicate handling and exudes no puffed up pretension. The pudding Christian is solid, empowered by a consistent faith built upon unceasing prayer, study of God's Word, humbled servanthood, and bending of will to God's purposes. "Pudding American Christianity." Life's roller coaster experiences may shake it, but nothing the destroyer designs can alter the sureness of its consistency or the firmness of its convictions.

Question for reflection: How firm is your faith - light as a soufflé or thick as pudding?

Spokespersons for the Word

Dear friends, do not believe every spirit, but test the spirits to see whether they are from God, because many false prophets have gone out into the world. This is how you can recognize the Spirit of God: Every spirit that acknowledges that Jesus Christ has come in the flesh is from God, but every spirit that does not acknowledge Jesus is not from God. This is the spirit of the antichrist, which you have heard is coming and even now is already in the world.

I John 4:1-3

The apostle John tells us exactly how we are to discern which of the myriad voices we hear today from pulpits across the land actually are spokespersons for the Lord. As believers we hold them up to the holy litmus test. Do they solidify their call to lead God's people by acknowledging unconditionally that Jesus Christ came in the flesh from God? If they do then they are authentic messengers of the one and only God. If they hedge, paraphrase, avoid, or ignore this truth and are unable to confess with their mouths this universal aspect of the faith or if they alter the words to suit their own biases, philosophies, or theological theories, then they are not from God. The Scripture says they represent the spirit of the antichrist in the world.

Hard to accept? After all Christian churches abound. In some places, there is one on almost every corner. And with the convenience of technology, you don't even have to "go" to church anymore. You can turn on the television or radio and catch some reverend preaching and teaching "twenty-four seven." No matter. Listen carefully and with discernment to their words. If any utterance is not consistent with God's Word, the Bible, it is not of God.

Question for reflection: What problems do you have accepting the Word of God as revealed in the Bible as His truth for humankind?

Strength + Courage = Obedience

"Have I not commanded you? Be strong and courageous. Do not be terrified; do not be discouraged, for the Lord your God will be with you wherever you go.

Joshua 1:9

Three times God tells Joshua to "Be strong and courageous" as He commissions him to lead the Israelites into the Promised Land following Moses' death. Nothing in the chronicles of events suggests that Joshua was hesitant, anxious, or afraid. Why then the Lord's repeated command for him to be "strong and courageous"? Perhaps Joshua, like us, needed to hear more than once that no matter what God has placed or allowed in our lives, we need not be fearful or fretful. He will not forsake us.

These words of encouragement that anchored Joshua in his obedience to God's call can do the same for Christian believers today. We may not be leading anyone to conquer new frontier land or territory, but as Christ's ambassadors, we are called to lead others to Him via the good news of the Gospel. And just as God knew the perils that Joshua would face, He knows the stumbling blocks and barriers, the resistance and even in some instances the dangers we will encounter as His witnesses. He sees the raised eyebrows of disbelief, the histrionic retorts and barbs, the veiled attempts to twist and alter the message of salvation, the blatant manipulation of truth toward socially accepted norms. So God speaks to us these same words of encouragement. Like Joshua, we need to hear them. As others see the strength and courage that mark our lives, they will come to understand we serve a God who is ever faithful, no matter the circumstances. Then one at a time, we will conquer the enemy's pitfalls as we strive in obedience to God's call.

Question for reflection: Is fear still holding you back from responding to God's call upon your life?

The Mystery of Disaster

I form the light and create darkness; I bring prosperity and create disaster; I, the Lord, do all these things.

Isaiah 45:7

Whenever disasters such as tornadoes, hurricanes, floods, earthquakes, car accidents, airline crashes, genocide or wars occur, there are always voices that cry out in anguish, "Why is God allowing this to happen?" Considering the pain and suffering such tragedies bring, the question is understandable. Even those who are deeply rooted in their faith may falter at such times and silently wonder, "Why, Lord? Why?"

It is precisely during these times of stress and challenge, that those of us who profess Christ Jesus as our Redeemer, must remember that we serve a complete God, a majestic, omnipotent God. A God who has formed and created everything. Within His scope of power are darkness and light, prosperity and ruin. He is a sinless shepherd who endured the horror of the cross before the glory of the resurrection. Even He who is the Son of God knew despair, suffering, pain, and sorrow. He accepted the dichotomy of the good and the bad as the divine unfolding of God's purpose and plan.

Does our claim of discipleship shield us from the dark side of life? Does it allow us to float unscathed by life's "slings and arrows" of misfortune? No, quite the contrary. Our discipleship gives us the strength, nurtured by faith and trust, to withstand the onslaught of disaster. It allows us to experience abundant, blessed living and to stand firm when the rug is snatched from beneath our feet.

As disciples of Jesus Christ, we don't have to ask "Why?" in any circumstance, whether prosperous or disastrous. We remain faithful servants of his will and purpose even when we don't completely understand them. We believe nothing occurs that has not first gone through him. And no matter how tragic situations seem to us, his purposes will be achieved through their unfolding.

Question for reflection: When disaster strikes, what does your response say about the state of your discipleship?

Things to Do

No one can serve two masters. Either he will hate one and love the other, or he will be devoted to the one and despise the other. You cannot serve both God and Money.

Matthew 6:24

The Visa card ad in the magazine caught my attention. Under the caption, "Things to Do While You're Alive" was a list of twenty-one activities we should experience during our life times. The implication being that these are things worth doing. The suggestions ranged from "Go to the Super Bowl and the Olympics" to "Take a train ride on the Orient Express and Climb Mount Olympus" to "Fly across the Atlantic in a private jet and Watch the Sumo Wrestling Championship in Japan." Like these, the other suggestions were expensive "to dos" requiring time and financial resources. Perhaps like most readers, my first reaction was to see how many of the things I had done, and secondly to ponder how many of the others were within my reach. I admit I was pleased with myself that I could check off two as memorable experiences. A few days later, I recalled the advertisement and reflected upon how each "thing" required a significant investment of money. To take the ad at its face value suggests a self-indulgent life style filled with the extravagant exploits commonly associated with the rich and famous. And perhaps the subliminal intent was that. To convince the reader that such a life would be richer, more fulfilling and exciting, a life well lived. Worthy of anyone's pursuit, right? Wrong!

Jesus understood the challenges his believers face in deciding the priorities for living. He taught that our hearts would be where our treasures are (Matthew 6:19-21). He explained to his followers how difficult it is to serve both God and the desires of the flesh. One or the other will eventually dominate (see Matthew 6:24). The magazine's man-authored list of desirable life experiences requires considerable amounts of money, the pursuit of which easily pushes us into the danger zone of serving the wrong master.

As disciples of Jesus, we cannot afford such pursuits. The call upon us demands we make choices that clarify which master we serve. I submit then an alternative list _ "The Christian's Things to Do While You're Alive". It brings back into focus who we serve and His expectations for the kind of lives we are to live.

- Donate the money you save by not attending the Super Bowl, the Olympics, or the Sumo Wrestling Championships in Japan to the Habitat for Humanity program to help them build houses for the poor and underprivileged.

- Volunteer the time you would have spent at those events at a Habitat for Humanity home site.
- Instead of spending time trying to "Hit a major-league fastball" or "Float along the Nile", become a mentor at a local public school and involve a young person in a little league program or science museum project.
- Use the money you would have spent on a "front-row center Broadway show ticket" or a "set of Frette linens" to adopt a family for the holiday seasons of Thanksgiving and Christmas.
- Rather than a "trip to the Galapagos Islands" for a carefree vacation, use the funds for the prison ministry of your church.
- Translate the time you would have spent "training like an astronaut at space camp" into volunteer time at the homeless shelter downtown.
- Take the funds you might have expended for "Gospel Brunch at the House of Blues" and buy canned goods for the homeless shelter's food pantry.
- In lieu of "going to the end of the earth", go to the hospitals and nursing homes and take a word of hope and encouragement, and a countenance of joy.

As the minister said yesterday, "Ease is the name of culture's game." Disciples of Christ do not live for themselves, nor do they seek lives filled with creature comforts and mindless entertainment. Theirs is a life of service offered to glorify God.

Question for reflection: What's on your list of things to do before you die?

Transforming Grace

*Do nothing out of selfish ambition or vain conceit, but
in humility consider others better than yourselves....
Continue to work out your salvation with fear and
trembling, for it is God who works in you to will
and to act according to his good purpose.*

Philippians 2: 3, 12-13

Once again, my devotional reading gives me pause.
The writer made the point that we enjoy getting credit
from others for the good deed we do and that is why
we tell them of our actions. I traveled mentally back to
an incident several years ago when I gave clothing to
a homeless woman in a post office parking lot. At that
time I was enrolled in a Disciple Bible study class. Each
session began with prayer and the sharing of individual
joys. I shared my encounter with the homeless woman
as a "joy" - an opportunity presented by God for
me to witness by my actions what He commands in
Matthew 25:36 (*I needed clothes and you clothed me...*).

The devotional piece made me ask myself the question, "Was I seeking recognition for my good deed by telling the class about it? Did anyone need to know?"

At the time I responded to the woman's obvious need, I felt I was moving out of my comfort zone to do something I had never done before. I could not ignore her as I had many others like her over years past. The joy I felt by responding as I did was too overwhelming to keep to myself, to keep a secret. My motive in sharing was not for recognition. I told of my deed because it was a "joy" to acknowledge how God was reshaping me to be the person He wants me to be. He was with me as I continued to work out my salvation according to His will and purpose. Should I have done the good deed and kept quiet? I don't think so. In this instance, my sharing of how God works in our lives when we allow Him to may have been just what a fellow believer needed to hear is possible on his journey to glorify our Lord and Savior.

Question for reflection: What good deeds have you done lately? Should you share them with others as a way of glorifying God?

Unceasing Forgiveness

*Then he said, "Jesus, remember me when you come
into your kingdom." Jesus answered him, "I tell you
the truth, today you will be with me in paradise."*
Luke 23:42-43

The scene is almost unimaginable. Three years of
urgent, compassionate ministry come to a halt at a place
called Golgotha, the Skull. Here is the Savior, God's
only son, Jesus, stretched out on a cross, enduring both
the physical pain and spiritual sorrow of a crucifixion.
Below Him the onlookers either vehemently taunt Him
or stand silently in resignation and despair. Adding
"insult to injury", His executors hang Him between
two convicted robbers, as if He too is only a common
criminal deserving of His fate.

Amazingly, as they hang there in agony, the three
have an encounter that only God could have orchestrated.
One of the robbers hurls insults at Jesus, demanding that
He save Himself and them as well. The other robber

rebukes his partner in crime, acknowledging their guilt and Jesus' innocence. Obviously believing, even in these circumstances, that Jesus is the Messiah, this robber asks the Savior for forgiveness and remembrance.

And what does our Lord do? Is His pain so unbearable that He focuses only on Himself? Is His heart so broken by betrayal and desertion that He hears only the slowing of His own heartbeat? Are His eyes so blinded by His blood and perspiration that He sees nothing but the darkness of impending death? Watch now. This great Lord we serve does the unbelievable. In pain and before He breathes His last breathe, He demonstrates the core of His ministry: repentance and forgiveness. He grants salvation to the robber.

What is the message here for us? If Christ in His final agony on the cross can forgive, so can we. Jesus shows us that forgiving others is something we do until death. Our physical and emotional conditions are never to be an excuse for not forgiving. We forgive because God has forgiven and continues to forgive us for debts we cannot repay. Someone has said, "We are born with a mortgage." And the only way it can get paid is by what Christ has already done through His death on the cross. We have received God's forgiveness by this act of sacrifice. So, we forgive. When the thief makes off with our prized possessions, we forgive. When the pedophile attacks our innocent child, we forgive. When the drunken driver runs down loving Aunt Susie, we forgive. When the mad gunman shoots indiscriminately into the crowd and cuts short the promise of a precious grandchild, we forgive. When the carjacker takes the family car and shoots our spouse in the process, we forgive. No matter how many times we are wronged, we forgive. "How can I?" you ask. "How can you not?" Jesus replies. "I forgave and forgive you daily. And you must do the same for others, if you are to be my disciple."

Question for reflection: When you are wronged by others, how difficult is it for you to forgive? What must you do to grow your ability to forgive in light of Christ's forgiveness?

Unconditional Praise

Praise the Lord. Praise the Lord, oh my soul. I will praise the Lord all my life; I will sing praise to my God as long as I live.

Psalm 146:1-2

Once again we wait. This time for a bone scan procedure. As we sit here in the hospital lobby area I reflect upon our ever-evolving circumstances and challenges. In the parking garage, my husband had asked, "Why are you so irritated?" I chose not to respond at that moment for fear of suffering "religion relapse", but mentally I played the tape of my morning to that point: discovery that the directions to our destination were not in the navigation system, miscalculation of the impact of the morning traffic, realization that the destination was clear across town past another medical facility to which we could have been referred, dizzying ascent in the parking structure in search of a vacant space, and bumbling along a maze of hospital corridors with too many directional signs. In the grand scheme of life, nothing really big, yet annoying enough to make me forget, momentarily, a cornerstone of my faith - praising the Lord anyhow, no matter the circumstances.

So let's push that replay button right now. Praise you, Lord, for the acumen to seek an alternative when the navigation system failed. Praise you, Lord, for allowing me to be in the traffic, but not burdened by the traffic as those may be who are on their way to work. Praise you, Lord, for the referral to a hospital world renowned for the quality of its patient services. Praise you, Lord, that the parking structure provides security and easy access to the elevators. Praise you, Lord, that you guided me to the right department with eyes to see and a mind to comprehend the directional signs. Praise you, Lord, this morning for you are worthy to be praised.

A preacher's comment in his Sunday sermon makes even more sense to me now. "It's your praise", he stated, "not your position that gets God's attention." My position this morning - getting to and now waiting at the hospital - will not in and of itself capture the Lord's attention, but my attitude and reaction to my position will. As Christians we must be ever mindful that God expects our praises and we are to never stop giving them. Whether simply annoyed by life's quirks or wiping away tears of sorrow, we are to praise our maker. When we praise, we honor God and demonstrate our trust and hope in Him. Our praise becomes our faith statement. It is this act of faith that causes Him to stop and say to us as He said to blind Bartimaeus who affirmed Jesus'divinity, "What do you want me to do for you?" (Mark 10:51). When we praise we affirm Him as Lord of our lives. And as our Lord He blesses us according to His will and purposes. Praise the Lord always.

Question for reflection: What should you do when you find yourself fuming and fussing and showing "attitude plus" if the Lord is indeed the Master of your life?

Unfaltering Faith

A few days later, when Jesus again entered Capernaum, the people heard that he had come home. So many gathered that there was no room left, not even outside the door, and he preached the word to them. Some men came, bringing to him a paralytic, carried by four of them. Since they could not get him to Jesus because of the crowd, they made an opening in the roof above Jesus and, after digging through it, lowered the mat the paralyzed man was lying on. When Jesus saw their faith, he said to the paralytic, "Son, your sins are forgiven.…. But that you may know that the Son of Man has authority on earth to forgive sins…" He said to the paralytic, "I tell you, get up, take your mat and go home." He got up, took his mat and walked out in full view of them all.

Mark 2: 1-5; 10-12

In this Scripture it is easy to focus on the paralyzed man and his miraculous healing. Perhaps more significant to the story however, is the point Jesus makes in verse five of the text: "When Jesus saw **their** faith, he said to the paralytic, "Son, your sins are forgiven."

Jesus acknowledged the faith of the friends before he turned his attention to the man. The unfaltering faith of these men brought them with their burden to Jesus, certain that he would meet the need. They were not discouraged by the difficulty in getting to Jesus; they didn't give up and say, "Well, at least we tried." No. They pressed on in faith to present their friend to Jesus for his healing touch.

How often are we moved to deliberate, specific action when the needs of others confront us? Does our profession of faith translate itself into being inconvenienced? To moving out of our comfort zones? Carrying that mat in a crowd was probably not easy; climbing onto the roof with the mat and cutting a hole was surely not convenient. The entire experience required the men to forget about themselves and concentrate instead on the needs of their friend. What moved them to these acts of compassion? This "out of the box" solution? Simple - their faith that if they did their part, Jesus would take care of the rest. Jesus' words confirm that they were right!

Question for reflection: As a believer, when has your faith led you to acts of kindness and compassion for others when it was not necessarily convenient?

Unmerited Riches

Lord, you have assigned me my portion and my cup; you have made my lot secure. The boundary lines have fallen for me in pleasant places; surely I have a delightful inheritance.

Psalm 16:5-6

These verses of Psalm 16 are a reminder that it is not by our merit, but rather God's grace that we enjoy many of life's accoutrements. The psalmist asserts that it is God who has provided for his needs, his security, and his future. He takes no credit for this good fortune. God alone is responsible for the blessings he enjoys.

Too often we believers who live in relatively secure environments with not just our needs, but also our wants more than satisfied, lose sight of this principle of our faith. We succumb to the god of self-sufficiency who feeds us the lie that we have what we have because we worked for and earned it. Enough time bowed before this imposter eventually convinces us that it is by our merit that we have come to this enviable station in life. The memory of God's graciousness that enabled our successes slips from our consciousness and spirit. We forget that He awakens us every morning, not because we did anything to deserve another day above ground, but because of His grace. We forget that it was God's grace that enabled our body, mind, and spirit to function in ways that led to our academic or career success. We forget that our riches are the evidence of His grace poured out for His purposes alone, not for our aims and desires.

As Christians, we must always remember there is nothing we can do to earn or merit God's favor. It is not our work, but His grace that saves us, that supplies our needs and most often our wants. Everything we have, everything we've accomplished is evidence of God's riches showered upon us by His grace. It is unmerited.

Question for reflection: Do you glory in the accolades or confess that God's grace is the reason for it all?

Waiting for the Results

...But those who wait for the Lord shall renew their strength...

Isaiah 40:31

Wait for the Lord; be strong and let your heart take courage; wait for the Lord.

Psalm 27:14

"Well, now, we just wait for the results." Familiar words. Each of us either utters or hears them at pivotal moments throughout our lives. In the spring, the preschooler takes a Readiness Test to qualify for fall admission to a top academy and we wait for the results. We send off the completed magnet school application for our culminating middle-school child and wait for the results. The four-hour SAT testing session concludes and our graduating senior waits for the results. The visit to the Women's Health Center for our annual mammogram ends (thank God!) and we leave to wait for the results. Just yesterday, as he emerged from the inner sanctum of the surgical center following a biopsy procedure, my husband's first words were, "Now we wait for the results."

On the drive home, I thought about the sentiment being expressed when we say, "We have to wait for the results." The words suggest our acknowledgement of having done all that we can do and the matter now is out of our hands. And if the situation is no longer in our hands, in whose hands does it rest? For the believer in Jesus, the Christ, the answer is simple. It's all in the Lord's hands and how we wait for the results mirrors our faith.

Believers turn to God's Word for guidance in how to wait for the results of any situation. The prophet Isaiah reminds us that waiting has its own rewards. Rather than depleting us of our energy, our hope, and our joy, waiting renews us. As we name and count our blessings during the wait time, we are invigorated by all God has done in our lives. Somehow the "results" take a secondary position and energetic praise moves to first chair. The psalmist urges us to be strong and courageous as we wait for the Lord. If it's in His hands, there is no cause for worry, anxiety, or fear. Rather, the waiting provides opportunity to demonstrate the tenacity of our faith. Prayerfully, in the strength of our Lord's promises, we "wait for the results" with dry hands, unfurrowed brow, and absolute trust "that the one who began a good work in you will carry it on to completion..." (Philippians 1:6). In other words, we wait with a confidence born from the belief that what's in God's hands is already handled. It just takes a little time for humans to get it recorded.

Reflection Question: When the inevitable "waiting for the results" moments crop up, what does your response say about your faith?

What Has Happened to Us?

However, if you suffer as a Christian, do not be ashamed, but praise God that you bear that name.

1 Peter 4:16

In Max Lucado's *Grace for the Moment*, he quotes from a letter written in the third century by Saint Cyprian to a friend. The writer shares that in the midst of their world's wars, oppression and cruelty, he found "a quiet and holy people...despised and persecuted, but they care not. They have overcome the world. These people are Christians." My immediate reaction to his depiction of these followers of Christ was to ask, "What has happened to us?" Honestly, would someone writing of today's western Christians use those descriptors? Could it be said we are "quiet", "holy", "despised", "persecuted" "over comers of the world"? In other words, are we set apart as Christ's followers in our current technological, profit driven, information-overloaded world?

Third century "quiet" can be translated as twenty first century "serenity". As Christians, how many of us live amidst the contemporary chaos with an observable spirit of serenity - calmness or peace- that others cannot explain? How successful are we in resisting the pull of the advertising frenzy that bellows "more, bigger, louder" are better? In the midst of the noise, the haste, are we indistinguishable from the nonbeliever?

As contemporary Christians, are we identifiable by our holiness in our decisions, our choices, our dreams, and our plans? Does our righteousness temper our responses? Or are we easily persuaded to "lay our religion down", to separate the church from the state, to demonstrate our faith only when in company of other believers rather than anywhere and everywhere we are in the world? As contemporary Christians do we give God the glory even when we are passed over for the promotion or raise by someone less qualified? Do we smile anyway when we are labeled "simplistic" or "naïve" because we attempt to live our faith in the open and not behind closed doors? As contemporary Christians are we ever mindful of God's purpose rather than man's design for our earthly existence? Do we demonstrate in even the mundane that this is not our home; we reside here temporarily as we press daily toward the promise of something more glorious - eternal life with Christ?

If a twenty first century observer of the contemporary Christian can not marvel at the lives we live as Christians in the midst of war, hunger, poverty, racism, sexual depravity, hatred, and all the other ills of modern society, then what has happened to us is we have lost the meaning of who we are and whose we are - a holy people, set apart by God for his glory. In the world, but not of the world. That's what has happened!

Question for reflection: What words would an observer use to describe your life as a modern day Christian?

When Will We Listen?

He said, "Go and tell this people: "'You will be ever hearing, but never understanding; you will be ever seeing, but never perceiving. This people's heart has become calloused; they hardly hear with their ears, and they have closed their eyes…." Then I said, "For how long, O Lord?"

Isaiah 6:9-11

In the sixth chapter of the book of Isaiah, God commissions the prophet to carry a hard and difficult message to a people who didn't think they had any religious problems - that they were on the Lord's "good foot" so to speak. Hearing the Lord's indictments against them, Isaiah asks how long they were to continue in their state of rebellion and sin. God answers him with a list of calamities that would eventually destroy the people, sparing a small remnant (Isaiah 6:11-13). Only after the nation has been annihilated, will they listen to God.

How keenly this Isaiah passage speaks to Christians today. So many of us claim the name of Christ even as we have ceased hearing him and perceiving his message for our lives. Because we practice to some degree the basic affirmations of our faith - church attendance, especially on Christmas and Easter, contributing financially, serving on a committee or with an organization - we don't think we have any religious problems. Ask us and we'll respond, "All is well with my soul." What we fail to grasp is how insidious the enemy has been in leading us to his alternatives and away from total surrender to God's truth. We have stopped listening to God because in our secular culture, we don't see the need. Not when we have so many more contemporary alternatives.

Consider how many "Christians" respond to life's challenges and uncertainties. We crowd our bookcases with the latest self-help edition no matter the perspective of the writer. Seldom do we remember to judge the content against God's standards. Whatever the relationship issue, we turn to these resources expecting them to make a difference in our situation. Or we spend countless hours browsing the internet for web sites that promise solutions and advice for anything that ails us. We even bookmark the sites for quicker access when the inevitable storms rage and once again we are caught in them. And when neither of these alternatives brings relief, we turn to the ubiquitous talk shows with their parade of troubled folk, just like us, who listen eagerly to the dispensation of media mogul wisdom. Turning to these alternatives rather than listening to our God eventually hardens our hearts to His call.

As true Christians, we must be ever alert to the danger of listening to man instead of God. He has given us all we need to face any life circumstance. As His followers, we go first to His Word, the Holy Bible, for the wisdom we need. When we yearn for talk and conversation about our situation, we seek His face and dialogue with Him in prayer. With our ears and eyes and hearts open to receive Him, we avoid hitting the walls of despair and ruin. The practice of listening to the Master for His guidance and direction sets us apart from the world's alternatives and positions us for God's blessings and favor.

Question for reflection: To whom or what are you listening for the answers to your challenges and concerns?

Where Are You?

But the Lord God called to the man, "Where are you?"

Genesis 3:9

You know the story. Adam and Eve disobeyed God in the Garden of Eden by eating fruit from a tree God had said was off-limits to them. Their actions yielded both newfound knowledge and feelings of fear and shame. Subsequently, when God came calling, they hid from Him. Now, we all know that God did not really have to call out, "Where are you?" In His omniscience, He already knew. They were where we all are when we turn from Him and follow our own desires and wills - the garden of despair, failure, and shame. He knew with this first man and woman as He knows with us that we cannot hide from Him. He seeks us though and keeps "a calling", wanting us to be in fellowship and communion with Him.

Adam and Eve came from behind the tree where they thought they were hidden. With denials and clumsy confession, they owned their sin, and God set in motion the unending mercy He extends, even as He meted out the consequences of their decisions. We experience the same today. He gives us salvation through His son Christ Jesus; we accept; we are tempted and turn away; with mercy He calls us back, extending His grace and forgiveness, even though we may still pay the price for our disobedience. For us, as it was for Adam and Eve, the key is that the call comes. "Where are you?" Despite our failures and feeble attempts to hide from Him, He continues to call, seeking to place us back in the place He had prepared for us from the beginning. In perfect relationship with Him.

Question for reflection: Are you where you should be when the Master comes "a calling"?

Where Would We Be?

Unless the Lord had given me help, I would soon have dwelt in the silence of death. When I said, "my foot is slipping," your love, O Lord, supported me. When anxiety was great within me, your consolation brought joy to my soul.

Psalm 94:17-19

Imagine the power of a musical collaboration between the writer of the Psalm and the contemporary artist who composed the lyrics, "If it had not been for the Lord on my side, tell me where would I be, where would I be?" Both the psalm and the gospel song remind us of the ultimate source of our help, the Lord who loves us. Such a collaborative effort might produce an antidote for our tendency to believe we can exist outside God's love and are the masters of our own fate.

Christian believers are challenged daily to resist the temptation to live outside God's love and go it alone. We live in a culture that applauds self-sufficiency and independence. Persons who appear to have built great wealth and fortune are held in high esteem. Society positions them as icons whose actions are guides to successful living. It is easy to fall prey to this mind set in our climb to the top of whatever mountain we are ascending.

The psalmist and the gospel lyricist remind us this is not the perspective of the believer. We know from whence our help comes. Without the Lord's support, our missteps and misguided efforts stop us in our tracks. Without His support and guidance, we exist as minions of anxiety and stress. Without His support, we feel no joy in our exploits, no peace with our acquisitions, no hope in our daily routines. Only when we surrender ourselves to the Lord of Life are we able to experience the certainty of where our help comes from. Our help comes from the Lord, the maker of heaven and earth. It is He who will not allow our feet to slip, who watches over us, who protects us from all harm (Psalm 121). The thought of where we might be without Him is too awful to contemplate.

Question for reflection: What would be the reality of your life now if the Lord had not been your help?

Whose Battle?

He said: "Listen, King Jehoshaphat and all who live in Judah and Jerusalem! This is what the Lord says to you: 'do not be afraid or discouraged because of this vast army. For the battle is not yours, but God's..."

2 Chronicles 20:15

Life is humming along with no discordant notes when out of the blue with no forewarning, the enemy's blazing arrows whiz straight at you. Your eighteen year old announces, "I'm gay. Deal with it." Your straight A sixteen year old weeps as she confesses she is pregnant and her boyfriend told her he is HIV positive. Your mother calls to say your dad has just had a heart attack and is on his way to the hospital. As you go into multi-task management mode, your mind races. What is going on? Why is all this coming at you now? How did you, a church going, praying mother, obedient daughter get caught in this crossfire? More importantly, what do you do about it? How do you bring sanity to seemingly insane circumstances like these? May I suggest the following?

First, you do a check of yourself to be sure that armor of God you put on when you came to Christ is still in place and not rusted away. Check that belt of truth around your waist; does it still fit or have years of compromising just the little things stretched it beyond recognition? Are you wearing your breastplate of righteousness or is it cast somewhere in the back of your spiritual closet, last seen beneath a pile of promises of faithfulness yet to be kept? Are your feet shod in the readiness of the gospel of peace or are you still prancing occasionally in your three-inch heels of conflict and confrontation? Is your faith shield positioned or have you forgotten how to hold it as you march daily in God's army holding up the "blood stained banner"? What about your salvation helmet? Snug on your head or hanging forgotten most days on the coat rack by the door? And that mightiest of weapons, your Spirit sword, God's unfailing, unerring word. Is it always in both your hand and your heart or do you remember you need it only in times like these?

If this check up reveals you are where God wants you be, then you are ready to confront these attacks. Remember, the Scripture tells us that the devil is always on the prowl seeking destruction and chaos. But when you are armed, he cannot deceive you with his arrows. You know the truth of God's Word. You know the righteousness that comes by faith. You know the peace that surpasses all understanding that He alone gives. You know that you walk not by what is seen but by faith for you serve a God who gives life to the dead and calls things that are not as though they were (Romans 3:17). You are ready to do now what Abraham did. You believe God's promises. You raised the children in the ways they should go and the promise is that when they are old they will not depart from these teachings. Your father's strong faith convictions have sustained him throughout life and the promise is that God will never leave or forsake him. You are a praying mother and daughter and the promise is that whatever you ask for in prayer is yours, if you believe.

Now is the time for you to surrender to God everything that may stand in the way of Him taking over this battle: your anxiety, your pain, your hurt, and your despair. You rejoice in praise as you freely yield the command post to Him. You stand aside as He takes on the enemy for the promise is that the battle is not yours, but His to fight and ultimately in His time to win. Glory to God. Alleluia.

Question for reflection: How do you know you are ready for the next attack of the enemy regardless of the direction from whence it comes?

Why Challenges?

…In this world you will have trouble. But take heart! I have overcome the world.

John 16:33

In his sermon, the preacher offered three reasons why God allows challenges in our lives: so we can glorify Him, so we can worship Him, and so we can praise Him. It was an inspirational and thought-provoking message. As I reflected upon it later in the afternoon, other reasons for why God allows challenges sprang to mind. I began to speculate on the reasons God may allow certain challenges at the different seasons of our lives.

In the formative years, most of us are encouraged by parents or significant others to complete our education and begin a career or job. We begin the climb toward the accomplishments society tells us will bring success and happiness. But often, just when we feel we are on top of everything, the challenges come, bringing chaos to our carefully designed plans. All of a sudden, we are no longer in control. The reins slip through our fingers and we stand confused trying to figure out what went wrong and why. It is in this season that perhaps God seeks to inform and remind us that we are to live according to His plan and will, not our own. He is in charge and the challenges we face force us to confront this reality.

As the years progress, silver streaks begin to highlight our tresses. Our climb to the top becomes the "back when" stories we tell over and over to our adult children and grandchildren. Our possessions spill beyond the confines of our home to lockers in the nearest storage facility. Yet, despite our outward appearance of success, real joy eludes us. There is little inner peace and no true sense of fulfillment. Perhaps this is the season of God's challenge of discontent in the midst of accomplishment. As we face the challenge, we come to understand that soul satisfaction comes only when we acknowledge that God alone gives life its meaning. Without Him at our center, all else is nothing.

Finally, the twilight fades to evening. The years take their toll and one health issue after another seems to define our days. After all this time, we wonder what we are still missing. We've lived through so much. Perhaps it is at this stage that God challenges us to unwavering obedience and complete submission to His will. He allows the struggles to push and stretch us beyond what we thought we could ever endure. In this final season of challenges, He reconciles us to Him in all His glory.

Question for reflection: Can you look at your challenges as just another way God may be trying to get your attention?

Wind and Faith

We live by faith, not by sight.
1 Corinthians 5:7

The more I reflect upon it, the more convinced I am that it was one of those serendipitous moments that mark our journey from time to time. That particular afternoon I sat on the deck, captivated by the sound of the wind as it moved through the tall oak and pine trees in our backyard. As the upper branches swayed to and fro, the resultant sound was a whispering noise almost magical in its effect. Not unlike the sound of waves crashing against the seashore. How, I thought, can something I can't see make such a peaceful melody? A few moments passed and I realized that though I can't see it with my naked eye, my experience of it confirms that it exists. I hear its whisperings, see its effect upon the trees, and feel it whenever it swirls around me.

That made me think of my faith; the foundation for my belief in what I can't see, but know beyond a doubt exists: Jesus the Christ, resurrected son of God who sits at our heavenly Father's right hand until the Day of Judgment. Like the wind, faith too is an abstract entity. I can't touch it as I can a rock or some other concrete object. Yet, I know it exists because of my experiences. As I *see* wind move the trees, I *see* faith sway the doubting mind to one that hopes and believes in God's promises. As I *hear* wind's whisper, I *hear* faith expressed in the gentle words of the septuagenarian testifying to God's grace and mercy. As I *feel* wind's touch upon my skin, I *feel* faith's power moving in the hearts of people, bringing calm to chaos and tranquility in the midst of tragedy.

Faith: an abstraction through the literal lens, concrete through the spiritual. Serendipity.

Question for reflection: Have you ever paused to allow God's natural world to speak to you of the truth of yours?

Wisdom's Call

*For whoever finds me finds life and receives favor
from the Lord. But whoever fails to find me harms
himself…*

Proverbs 8:35-36

Throughout the Book of Proverbs, the writer
personifies Wisdom as someone who, if you possess her,
will protect you, guide you, love you, and even honor
you. In short, those who acquire wisdom will reap the
benefits of an abundant life in God.

Upon reflection, it doesn't seem many of us today
accept this proverbial advice as pertinent. We do not
pursue Wisdom as a commodity upon which to build
our lives. Rather, we do just the opposite; we strive for
Wisdom's dividends without investing in her. The lure
of the material drives our labor. The accumulation of
things defines our status, our influence, and our worth.
Wisdom's desire to lead us to a life that finds favor with
God remains just that, her desire.

The Scripture tells us however, that when we fail to discover wisdom, we harm ourselves. Our relentless labor too often produces stress, broken relationships, heart attacks, and emotional meltdowns. The "stuff" of our lives ties us to blind trust in what we own rather than in He who made the provisions possible. Our sense of value is directly related to what we possess and we feel devalued when these things are lost or taken away.

We must remember that believers are held to higher standards. We are expected to heed Wisdom's call. In prayer we seek her, along with her companion, Understanding, because we trust God's word. We cry out for her because she promises that whoever listens to her "will live in safety and be at ease without fear of harm" (Proverbs 1:33). In wisdom there is life, not defined by the world, but by God. Abundant life lived in His favor.

Question for reflection: Do you seek Wisdom as the cornerstone for the life you live?

Your Highness, Self

Thou shall have no other gods before me.

Exodus 20:3

In verse two of Exodus 20, God reminds the Hebrew people who He is and of what He already has done for them. He is the Lord, their God, who led them out of bondage in Egypt. Then He gives them the laws He wants them to obey, the first of which is His commandment to have no other god before Him. Most of us recall how quickly the people forgot this commandment and convinced Aaron to build for them a golden calf, their own god to worship instead of God (Exodus 32:1a). We shake our heads in disbelief at how easily they turned to worship of a false god.

Unfortunately, many of us today, though we profess our Christianity, are strikingly like our biblical ancestors of Moses' day. We erect our "golden calves" - money, fame, possessions, power, and privilege and give them the reverence we know is reserved for God alone. And as our worship of these false gods begins to define who we are, a god even more dangerous ensnares us: self. Like the Hebrews who decided to make and rely upon a god they made, we come to believe more in ourselves than we do in God. Our wealth positions us to acquire not just what we need, but what we want. Our fame opens doors to opportunities we think we create. Our possessions set us apart as special and deserving of power and privilege. As these gods become more ingrained, we elevate "self" to godlike status. And as the Hebrews said of Moses, "As for this fellow Moses ... we don't know what happened to him" (Exodus 32:1b), the god "self" says today. "I don't know about God, but I've managed to make a way for my self. Look at who I am and all I have."

As contemporary Christians, we are reminded that God's Word is truth. What we sow, we shall surely reap. If we place other gods before the one true God, we throw away His promise of eternal life. But if we embrace His commandments, worship and trust Him alone as Lord of our lives, He extends His grace to us.

Question for reflection: Where is your allegiance? To God or to yourself?

Stand Still

Moses answered the people, "Do not be afraid. Stand firm and you will see the deliverance the Lord will bring you today. The Egyptians you see today you will never see again. The Lord will fight for you; you need only to be still."

Exodus 14:13

We can imagine the fear and absolute terror the Israelites felt as they beheld Pharaoh's army closing the gap between them and the Red Sea looming ahead. Trapped and hemmed in, their only recourse was to cry in despair to Moses, the one who had led them to this place. They faced a challenge beyond their capabilities to handle. There was nowhere to turn. When Moses replied and essentially told them to be still and watch God work, even the simplest among them understood this was their only option.

Likewise with us today. When the enemy has us boxed in, starring down a dark tunnel with no light at the end, we quickly cry out to God for deliverance. Then, we stand aside and wait for His rescue. That's all we can do. Standing still in the midst of life's big trials is not so difficult. The greater challenge often for us is practicing the same discipline when the "small stuff" crops up. For some reason, life's little cracks and flaws, annoyances and inconveniences upset us just as much and make standing still and waiting on the Lord a real challenge. Consider.

How crazed do we get dealing with the faults and imperfections of family, friends, and others? Are we constantly trying to fix what we perceive is broken: their habits, their attitudes, their choices, their opinions? What about the annoyances of the organizational systems that characterize the contemporary culture? Are we often fuming and fussing, ranting and raving at long lines wherever we go, bumper-to-bumper traffic, rising prices, shrinking resources, shallow politicians, or runaway technology? Though these challenges to our sanity and physical well-being may not measure as high on the Threat-to-Life scale as annihilation by an incoming nuclear weapon, they are nonetheless situations that we face best by "standing still".

We stand still and wait for the Lord's deliverance just as we would if our backs were truly against the wall. In prayer, we cry out to Him, seeking His face and trusting that He will not fail us. We relinquish our need to control to Him because we discern that only with Him in the lead will we be able to cope, whether the situation is overwhelming or a simple annoyance. With his grace to sustain us, we learn to stand still and follow him, even in the "small stuff" experiences.

Question for reflection: Think about your most recent "small stuff" experience. Were you able to stand still long enough to hear the Lord's leading?

Victory Is Ours!

When the perishable has been clothed with the imperishable, and the mortal with immortality, then the saying that is written will come true: "Death has been swallowed up in victory." "Where, O death is your victory? Where, O death is your sting?"

I Corinthians 15:54-55

A sister-in-Christ died this week. We were classmates in the long-term Disciple Bible study program at my former church. During the fourth and final year we worked in the same small group. Each Thursday evening she sat to my right at our table brightening our time together with her infectious smile, optimistic outlook, thoughtful questions, and wonderfully humorous, common sense remarks. I was saddened when I heard several weeks ago that she was gravely ill. In concert with many others, I had been praying for her healing and recovery. During the past several years the Lord

221

has answered my prayer petitions so often with a, "Yes, I'll do that." the idea that He might not do the same this time was not a conscious thought. As believers often do, I forgot that the Lord answers our prayers in one of three ways: with a "yes", a "wait", or a "no". My experiences of His affirmatives had lulled me away from my understanding that we pray to Him for everything while acknowledging what we really want is His will and not our own to be manifested.

After several minutes of digesting the news of her death, my mood shifted from sadness to joy as I realized that she had made the glorious transition and reached the destination all believers journey toward. She was absent in the body, but present with the Lord. She was home for good! No more pain. No more suffering. No more sorrow. Tears of anguish wiped away. This was a time of celebration for all who claim Christ as their Lord and Savior.

Those four years of study, reflection, and growing understanding of God's Word sprang to life. My sister-in-Christ's death is a reminder that we serve a God who loves us and yes, wants to satisfy the desires of our hearts. But he is more significantly a God who has always known the plans he had for each of us. Ultimately, he is in control and when his purposes for the believer's life have been fulfilled, he bestows his reward: "Well done, good and faithful servant… Come and share your master's happiness" (Matthew 25:23). What then are we to conclude when God allows Death's arrow to hit its target? We do not linger long in the darkness of despair because the perishable is no more. We accept that there is both a time to mourn and a time to wipe away the tears as we embrace the joy of a new morning. Finally, we rejoice in the love of our Heavenly Father whose son, Jesus Christ, has given us victory over death. Our Savior who has promised there is a place already prepared for us when we get home. Carried gently on angelic wings, my sister-in-Christ has crossed the finish line into the Savior's waiting arms. All believers rejoice in her victory!

Question for reflection: Are you able yet to see death as a time to celebrate the believer's victory and arrival home?

Submit, Shake, Serve

Submit yourselves, then, to God. Resist the devil, and he will flee from you.

James 4:7

A somewhat trendy message is emanating from our pulpits and choir lofts in churches these days. In both word and song, we hear the admonition to "shake the devil off." This catchy phrase might be considered too secular for some, but I submit that there is merit in this contemporary expression. It captures our attention and if really understood can help us resist the devil's designs upon our lives. In fact, the Scriptures proclaim the same message, just in different words. Listen to Jesus in these verses from the Gospel of Matthew (4:10-11): *...'Away from me, Satan! For it is written: 'Worship the Lord your God and serve only him'.' Then the devil left him...* A verbal "shaking off" for sure! This Scripture, the one above from the book of James and our catch-phrase "shake the devil off" remind us that we are to be proactive in curtailing the devil's influence. How? Glad you asked.

First, we learn to speak God's Word into every situation. Doing this reminds us that we are called to worship and serve only one God. We shout a resounding, "NO", to any temptation. We proclaim victory in Jesus' name as we watch the devil slink away from us. Secondly, we submit our wills to God's will. As we do this more consistently, our power to resist the lures of the devil increases. And as our resistance to him grows, we discover his influence weakens and he retreats from us. Finally, as the ditty proclaims, we literally "shake off" all the stuff the devil throws on us: doubt, fear, anxiety, confusion, lost focus, whining, envy, immorality, hatred. We shake these imposters off with greater prayer, praise, thanksgiving and worship of our God. We understand that the devil cannot cling to us when we practice these disciplines and they define who we are and whose we are. So go ahead. Submit to the Lord, shake off the devil at every turn, and serve the Lord until Satan's influences are banished forever.

Question for reflection: Have you learned to "shake the devil off" or is he still riding your shoulders, influencing your every turn?

Salt Water Tongues

Can both fresh water and salt water flow from the same spring? ...Neither can a salt spring produce fresh water.

James 3: 11-12

When reading chapter three in the book of James, we often focus on verses nine and ten - "With the tongue we praise our Lord and Father, and with it we curse men, who have been made in God's likeness. Out of the same mouth come praise and cursing. My brothers, this should not be." Today, for some reason, verses eleven and twelve captured my attention. The question and declaration of these verses are clear. If there is salt in a spring, nothing fresh will emerge from it. A fitting analogy for our tongues. A sharp, negative, cynical, abrupt, spiteful, boastful, lying, foul tongue is a salt-spring tongue. Such a tongue will never produce anything fresh. Galatians, chapter five, instructs us to live by the Spirit. The fruit of this Spirit - love, joy, peace, patience, kindness, goodness, faithfulness, gentleness and self control – can not be produced from a "salt spring." These virtues require "fresh water" to flow. Salt water tongues will not do the job.

As Christians we are called to produce with our tongues the "fresh water" of spiritual fruit, to utter words that flow easily and satisfy the spiritual thirst of all to whom we speak. As Christ's disciples, we are challenged daily to be intentional in using our tongues to bless, not curse, to heal not destroy, to encourage not hinder, to calm not enflame. We do this by filtering the saltiness out of our words so that the freshness of God's Spirit can be heard by those inclined to listen.

Question for reflection: Is your tongue doing double duty?

What is Truth?

"You are a king, then!" said Pilate. Jesus answered,
"You are right in saying I am a king. In fact, for
this reason I was born, and for this I came into the
world, to testify to the truth. Everyone on the side
of truth listens to me."

"What is truth?" Pilate asked.

John 18:37-38

Taken before Pilate, the governor of Rome, to answer the charges brought against him by the Jewish leaders, Jesus concludes his comments to Pilate with the words, "Everyone on the side of truth listens to me." And in one of his defining moments, Pilate, before turning away from Jesus and addressing the crowd intent upon crucifixion, responds with the universal question, "What is truth?"

Like Pilate, we too turn away from the answer - Jesus - and equivocate on the issue. Depending upon the situation, we define truth to suit our circumstances. And of course, truth loses its clarity when we decide one's truth is as valued as another. In the end this kind of thinking reduces truth to nothingness.

For Christians, there is but one truth, Jesus Christ. What He said and all He did define truth for us. We find our sense of truth in his words and his deeds. John sums it up in the fourteenth chapter when Jesus states, "I am the way and the truth and the life." Not sure if what you profess or proclaim is truth? Test it against God's Word. Does it hold up? If it doesn't, it is not truth. It is a lie.

Question for reflection: What do we do when the truth we are called to speak brings pain or denial?

Acknowledgements

I could not have completed this book of devotions had it not been for God's angels hovering over me and whispering words of encouragement and inspiration. Often when I wrote, I felt completely overwhelmed by the Lord's Spirit. All praise and honor and glory belong to God alone. As He knows, this was Him allowing me to use the gift He gave. I tried to use it in obedience.

I thank family and friends who have listened to the reading of many of these devotionals over the years and continually offered their encouragement for me to "finish the book".

In gratitude I shout, "Thank You, My Sisters", to Dianna and Donna for reading the manuscript in its entirety and blessing me with their critical eye to its content and theology. I am indebted to them for their willingness to give time and effort to this project. I am also grateful for the patient technical assistance provided by my son,

Quentin. His perseverance, when mine failed, enabled the completion of this effort. Thank you, son.

Finally, with tears behind my eyes, I acknowledge the faithfulness of my now departed husband, Earl. It was his joy to be my "first hearer" each time I finished a piece. He was my most ardent encourager and had looked forward so eagerly to the book's publication. "It's done, dearest heart."

About the Author

For close to 40 years, Beverly Clopton worked first as public school English teacher and then a senior high school administrator in Dallas, Texas, Denver, Colorado, and Los Angeles, California. A professed Christian since age 8, Beverly had passed the half century mark before, she says, " I clearly understood what it meant to be in personal relationship with the Lord." Her "pentacostal" experiences while enrolled in the *Disciple* Bible study program opened her eyes to how she could better be about Kingdom business. Utilizing her gift of teaching, she became a *Disciple* facilitator in 2002. During that same period, she gave greater attention to what she calls her primary gift - writing. For years she had filled journals with her God inspired reflections and meditations on scripture. In 2007, she made the decision to turn those journal entries into a book of devotions. In sharing these pieces with friends and women around the nation who call into a weekly prayer line, she was encouraged by their responses that what she wrote was what women (and men) needed and wanted to hear. *Heaven or Bust...* is the result.

Currently, Beverly is working on a second book that chronicles her "walk through the valley" upon the sudden death of her husband of 29 years. She lives in the Atlanta area with her son and his family.

Printed in the United States
137022LV00001B/3/P